God Saved My Bipolar Butt

Though Ravaged by Mental and Physical Illness,
God Made Me into a Man of Peace

John W. Wenzler

John W. Wenzler

First Edition

God's Grace Publishing LLC
Milwaukee, Wisconsin USA

God Saved My Bipolar Butt

Though Ravaged by Mental and Physical Illness, God Made Me into a Man of Peace

Published by:

God's Grace Publishing LLC
3600 N. 96th Street
Milwaukee, WI 53222
www.godsgracepublishing.com

Scripture taken from the New King James Version®. Copyright © 1982 by Thomas Nelson, Inc. Used by permission. All rights reserved.

The name Slide Hampton® used by permission.

This book was printed in the United States of America
Copyright © 2012 by John W. Wenzler

First Printing 2012

Library of Congress Cataloging-in-Publication Data
Wenzler, John W.
God saved my bipolar butt: though ravaged by mental and physical illness, God made me into a man of peace/by John W. Wenzler, 1st ed.

ISBN 978-0-9853074-0-0 (pbk.)

Library of Congress Control Number 2012937562

TABLE OF CONTENTS

ACKNOWLEDGEMENTS

Sincere thanks to so many people who made this book happen.
My best friend and ex-wife Karrie, edited and re-edited every
sentence, and made the project a saleable book.
Her knowledge of self-publishing
allowed this to happen with almost no money.
Kathy, my dear friend, edited grammar and fine details.
Lisa, my talented niece, created the cover. After our confusing
direction, she delivered the bold, simple message we needed.
My heartfelt thanks to my mom and my dad
for their support of the project.
Mom died during the writing of this book,
I think she would have been proud of the result.

My appreciation to the many people who read the book
in it's early stages. You provided feedback and
encouragement when I needed that to keep going.

Most importantly, thanks to God for allowing me to
focus and not quit. His spirit gave me
patience with the process.
It was a healing process, I am thankful.

*First, I thank my God through Jesus Christ
for you all, that your faith is spoken of
throughout the whole world.
Romans 1:8*

INTRODUCTION

This book is not only about the ravages of mental illness, or the pain and disability of physical illness - though my stories are about such struggles. This book is about how I surrendered before God through experiencing intense levels of physical pain and the emotional fatigue and confusion of mental illness. I had to call on God's strength and power as I had none of my own.

My story is more importantly about how God allowed me to become a man of peace in spite of these things. My story is about how my faith along with God's grace and mercy has blessed me and guided me through it all.

I haven't told my story chronologically. Rather, I wrote as I remembered and thought about the different events, people, feelings and above all, blessings. The organization, like my confusing mental illness and chaotic life makes sense most of the time. I have grouped stories that make a similar point so that if you wish to read a random chapter or story, that you might experience encouragement or learn something interesting by reading randomly if you wish.

Chapter 1: Manic Adventures

My God will meet all your needs
according to his glorious riches in Christ Jesus.
Philippians 4:19

I had no idea how God would meet all my needs during those episodes when my mental illness would make horrible decisions on my behalf, decisions that caused great loss and hardship. I now look back on many events where God's hand owned all my ways. My faith opens me up to see, focus on, and be thankful for all the blessings God has for me. My faith shows me how his timing has guided me – even in the worst of my psychiatric and medical horrors.

Magic Manic Spending

When I'm manic, I'm able to somehow make large purchases without money. Without a down payment, with my lousy credit, and at times without any employment, I make large purchases. From hundreds of dollars to tens of thousands of dollars, my mind, when manic, thinks I have it to spend.

In the spring of 2010, I went for a leisurely drive, in search of a lake. I ended up in a country-like area, Mukwonago. I was about 30 miles southwest of Milwaukee. I saw a house for sale and knocked on the door. The woman invited me in and showed me the house. We visited for a long time, and I had her convinced that I could put $20,000 down and buy the house. I pestered this poor woman almost daily for weeks, she thought I was going to buy her house.

My brain truly thought that I was going to make a million dollars from the music concert that I was working on. I was sure that I would be buying her $800,000 lake property. When my ex-wife found out about this from a flyer in my car, she called the woman and her real estate agent to explain what was really going on. They got very angry with her for interfering with the transaction. I can be very convincing.

For years I liked to spend money impulsively on my businesses. In spring 1989, I was 33 years old. As usual for no reason and without any money, I decided that I wanted to look at a new truck for my company. I thought I would just browse around a car lot. I walked around and came across a Nissan King Cab pickup. Inside looked like an airplane cockpit, I was very impressed. The salesman invited me inside and introduced me to his manager. Ripe for the picking, manic and impulsive.

Of course I was told they were having a special that day which would allow me to buy it with no money down. Next was the question of collateral. I somehow talked them into accepting my worthless five-year-old carpet cleaning company as collateral. (I become a convincingly believable salesman with all the right answers and right timing when I am manic). Just like that, I drove off driving that pickup for $375 a month. My impulsive irrational brain had not thought for a minute about how I was going to make the monthly payments.

The Stakes Get Higher $$$

The next day I drove to the company that supplied my vehicles and equipment. The owner saw my new pickup. I had already purchased two used Isuzu trucks and other supplies there in the past. He said, "John, you must be doing great in your business to have purchased a truck like that."

He offered to sell me his 25-year-old, profitable business for $150,000. I hate these types of memories – if only I had not been manic when I bought his company. Another thoughtless impulsive purchase, these are always expensive. Financial suicide. At the time, I had grown tired of always trying to find new clients. I thought if I had his company added to mine we would always be busy. I dreamed of no more marketing, just scheduling.

I rushed into the deal without the counsel of an accountant or attorney. I offered 25% of gross receipts of both businesses as payment towards the deal. This was stupid and made no sense – the offer was at or above my normal profit margin, so I was giving him all of my expected profit or more. No money down, yeah what a deal. In the transaction I inherited his $1300 Yellow Pages monthly bill which was another nail in the financial coffin every month. The three truck mount vehicles that I leased from him had constant problems, repairs about $500 a month each. I added a phone line and tried to move forward. Mania makes me think that anything is possible, no – it makes me think that impossible things are possible. They don't call this insanity for no reason. That was fall 1989.

There was not much work coming from the business I purchased. Soon it was the slow season of winter, and my brain did the annual swing into depression, such horrible darkness. So there I am in January, suicidal, hopeless, employees laid off, driblets of work coming in. Depression zapped any energy or desire to do anything about it. I was a wet dish rag with a business going down the tubes – one that never really had a chance of succeeding in the first place.

God's Perfect Timing

God's timing, in my experience, is what happens in the high and often psychotic stages of mania. Everything works. When I stop to see someone without an appointment, they would be there. My sales went way up, everyone buys.

Once, when I was in my early thirties, I sold over $60,000 of work in three weeks. I have not been able to do that since. It was not my doing, God orchestrated the events. I was on local television for a news demonstration for one of our services. I was in the right place at the right time. When I am in the heaven of mania, I feel I live in a perfect world and nothing can go wrong. There is evidence to support my feeling, things like the free television PR is proof to me that I am in a perfect world. Sadly, I am also convinced at the time that it will continue. I feel invincible. Mania is fun at these times.

What money I did make, I often spent on alcohol, pot, and women. I did not understand anything, my life was a mess, caused by my horrible bipolar brain making me do things I would never choose to do, things I would never do when stable.

When I walked away from that business I had to give up the office. I also had to give up my living space, the flat that I remodeled with my manic high energy and my own money. I lost the Nissan King Cab and other vehicles. I had to sell off what I owned and agree to pay $25,000 back to the state in payroll taxes that I had forgotten to file.

Having no money and no car, I bartered for one with International Monetary Systems (IMS) dollars that I had left over from a client payment. Again, a gift from God that could not be taken away in the liquidation as it was otherwise worthless paper. I was able to get an old Buick that used a lot of oil. I loaned it to a friend. He ran it dry, and I was without a car. Then the despair, the dark winter season of suicide took over at this same time. All is hard and hopeless.

Manic Driving Adventures

I have always enjoyed driving. I drove as a courier for six years, four of those years as a truck driver. I was in my late 30's. I truly loved it, getting paid to do something I enjoyed, and I was good at it. What a blessing. I enjoyed being six feet up in the air where I could look over the vast landscape. God watched out for me during those years. I never had a manic episode during my employment as a driver. I can't imagine the mayhem that could have happened to me and others, especially my employer. God protected it all, I am grateful for that season of normalcy and stability, I enjoyed it.

When I am in a state of mania, I get myself in trouble by either driving for too many hours, or I start out with very little sleep, little gas, or all of the above. The end result is that my reasoning becomes confused and irrational. I make impulsive decisions. I drive extremely fast, I drive recklessly without realizing it. I start out driving and end up some place far away that was not in the plans. Sometimes I even think that God will allow me to keep driving on an empty gas tank. I ignore that I am out of gas and drive until the car stops. My brain ignores that there is no money in the bank to buy more gas with. AAA is not happy when you call them on a regular basis for a rescue with a can of gas.

I am not making these choices, my brain is ill and not working properly, it makes me do such confusing and unexplainable acts. I really hate when people blame me for these acts as if I would choose such whacky behaviors. The phrase 'losing my mind' is a truly accurate term at these times.

Appleton Dumpsters

On one manic drive when I was 45 years old, I drove in my carpet cleaning van overnight from Milwaukee, Wisconsin to somewhere in Michigan for no particular reason. I never need a reason or a destination when manic, I just go and go, I drive and drive.

On my way back to Milwaukee, I stopped in Appleton, Wisconsin. I was so tired from lack of sleep and driving all night, that my mind misinterpreted a Bible verse.

My faith in God and his presence in my life is so strong. However, when I enter into a manic state of mind, my spirituality goes off the charts. This is where faith and spirituality turns into psychotic religiosity. When it has happened, I am so emotional that I read the Bible and weep. I sob with hysteria because God shows me many profound things. My mind twists to odd reactions, including being convinced that I am Jesus Christ.

When I am stable and normal in my thinking, I have an inner confidence that comes from my deep faith. With that, I also carry inner peace of mind. When I am level in my thoughts, I read the Bible daily by praying before I open it. I am led to a verse that is perfect for that day or that moment. I reflect on it, meditate on it a bit, and often use that information in my e-mail encouragement ministry for others to read during their day. My understanding and interpretation could be described as 'quite normal'.

When I am manic, these thoughts are multiplied times ten. It causes confusion and leads to disarray. When mania is controlling my brain, I read the Bible and I take the verse too literally. I actually feel like I am living in times of the Bible and Jesus is speaking to me personally. My sense is that as I read the verse, Jesus is coming up out of the Bible to sit across from me and make commands. I misinterpret what I am reading and take impulsive action. My action is based on a strong irrational pull that I must obey God's command and instruction. The pull is so strong to obey, that I will go to extremes to obey.

Back to events in Appleton: -- I stopped at a gas station that was closed for the night. I drove to the back of the building. I was desperate to rest my eyes and try to stop the racing thoughts in my brain that were keeping me awake. I noticed two dumpsters in the alley and parked near them to conceal my van from the street. I was paranoid that someone would see me there. I got comfortable and closed my eyes, I unsuccessfully tried to sleep. I was nervously paranoid being parked there, so I decided to reach for my Bible. I opened the Bible randomly, and it revealed what I asked for. However, the meaning is skewed when my mental illness is driving my brain irrationally.

Behind the gas station, I opened up my Bible and read this verse: ***Trust in the Lord with all your heart, and lean not on your own understanding; in all your ways acknowledge Him, and he shall direct your paths.***
Proverbs 3:5-6

My mind, playing manic tricks on me, allowed me to misunderstand the verse. I thought it was commanding me to lean on God with His understanding because I had no clue what my own understanding was. In my elevated manic state I perceived that I needed to trust God with my life, literally in every way. I was going through a divorce that I had just manically asked for and nothing made sense. What I thought that God wanted was for me to show Him that I trusted Him with everything I owned by throwing away my possessions.

I unloaded everything I had in the van into the dumpsters next to me. I quickly pulled out my carpet cleaning portable machine with wand and hoses. Next, all of my supplies and chemicals, all went into the dumpster. I no longer recall why, but I had my precious trombone and sheet music with me. It all went into the dumpster.

I was extremely emotional, I feared that God wanted every last thing from me. I placed my wallet including credit cards and money into the dumpster too. I sat in my van sobbing uncontrollably and pleading with God, asking why He wanted to take so much from me when I had so little. I prayed to God, thinking of Jeremiah 33:3 which says, ***Call to me, and I will answer you, and show you great and mighty things, which you do not know.***

In my manic state, I thought I was showing God that I trusted him by giving up all my belongings. I was comforted by my memory of this Bible verse, knowing that I did not have to understand my decision or what would come next. God would.

As it happened, God was already working to create great and mighty things that I was unaware of. An employee of the gas station called my wife from one of my business cards found in my wallet out of the dumpster. The employees were concerned that I was robbed or something worse. The employees took everything out of the dumpster and saved it.

My wife contacted my parents. It just so happened that my brother was in Appleton for business the next day. Coincidence? I believe that only God's grace and timing makes such circumstances. My brother stopped at the gas station the next day and collected the items which included every little item that I had put into the dumpster except one piece of equipment.

The next morning I woke up in total fear for what I had done. I was told by my parents in the afternoon that everything was safely coming back to Milwaukee. My father reassured me, "God was good to you today, you trusted Him and He returned everything back to you, even your wallet and credit cards. He seems to want you to stay in business." At the time it was my entire identity to run my little business, and I was good at it. I played rare jazz gigs with my trombone, but I was not good enough to make a living with my horn.

Those 'Crazy' Pain Medications

One fine spring I felt an uplifted energy coming on. I was 54 years old this time. That's a nice way of saying another spring manic episode was revving up in my brain. I had many stable years on medications, so what happened this time?

I went to my pain specialist for an appointment. I told him that the medication he had prescribed was no longer controlling my severe neuropathy pain that resulted from brain surgery years earlier. He doubled what I was taking. I tried the double dose for two weeks and did not feel any relief, so I stopped taking that medication entirely. Two weeks later we met and he recommended biofeedback. I went to one appointment and my insurance would not cover it.

I was in trouble. No medications, severe pain. I later discovered that the medication I had been taking acted as a depressant. Therefore, going on a double dose, then off of it, put me up into a manic. I now know that many pain medications affect my mental illness severely. Either the meds are sedating and inducing suicidal depression, or there is an anti-depressant affect creating mania. This would have been helpful to know during all my medical hospitalizations when I was swinging out of control either high or low.

A few days later, I woke up during the night at my ex-wife's house with an intense charlie horse in my right calf. It was so severe that I could not move my leg or walk. Paramedics came and took me to the emergency room. The first thing they tried was Morphine. Without much delay, Valium. Eventually I got up off the table and walked off the constant spasms.

The damage had been done. I went from feeling the pain to feeling euphoric quite quickly. My body and mind for some reason react opposite to many chemicals. For instance, Ativan and Ambien in large doses make me psychotically manic instead of sedated. The drugs that day in the hospital threw me quickly into a higher manic. This jump upwards started weeks of poor decisions that were dangerous to my medical conditions, my finances, my life. Yes, the mania is just as life threatening as the depression part of bipolar.

So, when I was released from the hospital I was so high that I forgot to take my daily meds entirely. I missed my three bipolar medications as well as my medically necessary pills. Lithium, Depakote, and Zyprexa was my psych cocktail at the time. I also stopped taking my heart med, Metoprolol and my blood thinner, warfrin.

He Doesn't Have Pain – He's Crazy

In the days and weeks after the charlie horse episode, I was rushed by paramedics five times to different local emergency rooms due to my severe pain. My manic mind at the time did not even consider that not taking my blood thinner would result in new blood clots developing on top the old blood clots in my legs, or clots that could land in my brain or lungs and kill me. Clots forming in my legs was part of what created the new pain that was way off their zero to ten pain scale.

These emergency rooms did not do ultra sound scans on my legs or try to determine the cause of the pain, even after explaining my medical history and admitting to being off my blood thinner. When one is mentally ill, that's all medical pros focus on. It is assumed that I am either drug seeking or my pain is 'in my mind.'

I took the pain medications, when I was given any, at the hospitals. I was given shot or a pill and sent on my way, but no one ever issued a prescription. Therefore, the pain continued to severe extremes. One hospital gave me shots of Haldol, which again should have calmed me down and didn't do a thing. At least they tried something.

Chapter 2: A Manic Mess, Unlike Any Other

Surely the Lord our God has shown us His glory
and His greatness,
and we have heard His voice from the midst of the fire...
Deuteronomy 5:24

Time to Go, Gotta Go, - Where? Why?

    One morning in the spring of 2010, I decided to stop over at my ex-wife's for a bite to eat. When I've been manic around her, I either hate her and file for divorce or love her and want to be around her, only extremes and always impulsive. She had made breakfast for me this particular morning but all I ate was the bacon. She later admitted to crushing Depakote and Zyprexa into the scrambled eggs in a desperate attempt to stabilize my insane behavior.

    I was eating as little as a meal a day. I lose my appetite when I'm manic, it does not cross my mind to stop and eat, always gotta go, and then gotta go somewhere else. As such, after eating the bacon, off I went for a Sunday drive to Skokie, Illinois. When I arrived at my friend's home, I was told he was in Indiana at a music rehearsal. So I drove to Indiana to meet with him. I never call ahead, I just go places and assume the people will be there – rude, impulsive, yes.

    In the 33 years that I've known my friend, I had never driven to Indiana to see him. It was the craziest thing to do. I had literally been functioning on three hours per day of sleep at most because of my neuropathy pain. Mania not only gives me constant, relentless, extreme energy. Even when I lay down, I cannot shut off my thinking. A circus running many things at one time in my mind, like trying to sleep at a crowded rock concert – not gonna happen.

My mission was to drive to get away from home. Home was chaos. Actually, it was all caused by me, but at that time I was convinced it was all them! Them, meaning anyone that wasn't me. Such lack of self awareness, it's just strange.

When I arrived in Indiana my friend told me I could not meet with him. So, I decided I was going to drive to New York City. All I had was the clothes on my back, still wearing my bedroom slippers.

That night I arrived in Detroit and the freeway came to an abrupt end in the direction I needed to go. I called my father, always a navigator with maps. He referred to a map, then told me I would have to drive south to Toledo, then go east. So of course I did not listen to him, I drove north thinking somewhere I could go east. An hour and a half later I called dad and he got out his maps again. He found that I was on the west side of Lake Huron and it was best to go back south to Toledo to the interstate. I pulled over and slept for an hour then continued my journey south.

So, How Did I Get into Toronto?

After my rest and more driving, I determined I missed the Toledo exit and went back to Detroit. In my delirium, I looked at the lit up bridge that goes into Canada. It was glowing, like sunshine or heaven maybe. I was convinced it was the correct way that God wanted me to travel. I crossed the bridge and came up to a hut with an immigration sheriff in it. We talked for quite awhile and he finally asked, "what do you declare?" and I replied, "two packs of cigarettes." He told me to proceed to the immigration building. I did not have a passport or birth certificate, and I had marijuana in the glove box of my car.

As I entered the building I was wearing my sheepskin bedroom slippers and my smelly, dirty pants. Earlier in the trip when I entered Indiana, I felt a gurgling in my stomach and for over 30 minutes the bacon I ate for breakfast took over and filled my pants numerous times before I could find a gas station or way side. I eventually pulled over at a rest stop and threw away my filled underwear. I did the best I could to clean my pants, well you get the picture.

So, I walk into immigration with a stench. I went to the last booth and was asked even more questions. I told them I was a jazz trombonist on my way to New York City to buy a new trombone at a place I had worked at in the 80's. His last question was, "if you had to go back to the U.S., how would you get there?" I explained, "my dad would fly in with my birth certificate and I would be able to drive back." No suitcase, no change of clothes, not even a toothbrush, no shoes, and no birth certificate. He let me drive into Canada. Huh?

Call upon Me in the day of trouble;
I will deliver you, and you shall glorify Me.
Psalm 50:15

Lost in a Maze

Now in Canada, I stopped at a gas station and bought Lemon Pledge. I sprayed it all over my seat and car. It didn't work. My car smelled like a piece of furniture with a dirty diaper in it. I found out the best way to go was through Montreal. That's where I drove to, until I was stopped on a bridge. I looked down and the entire freeway system for miles in all directions was stopped. Lack of sleep was catching up with me. I decided go south thinking I would figure out how to head west back home. All of a sudden it hit me. I was in serious trouble without a birth certificate to get out of the country, so I became extremely anxious and paranoid.

I called my dad, told him that I finally understood what the whole trip was about: To trust God when I am lost. Not knowing where I was, I was afraid. I was an illegal alien and I was now running out of gas. Fear ripped through my thoughts and I began to cry, terrified that I had gotten myself into a heap of trouble.

Called my navigator again, dad and I prayed for deliverance. I told dad where I thought I was. I saw that the freeway would split two lanes to the left and two lanes to the right, time after time. I am normally excellent at knowing what direction I am going when I am driving, this time I was going in circles and did not know east from south or west or whatever. The prayer helped calm me even if I was still lost.

Only in mania would I be convinced that four is a spiritual number, 40 as well. For it is, the Trinity and me. So I entered freeway 40 and dad found it on his Canadian map. He said it was the correct way to go to head back west to home. Even in mania I am close to God and receive His blessings. I didn't want to imagine what would have happened to me if I ended up out of gas on the interstate in my delirium. Not to mention the stench, the pot, and of course no passport.

I remember it was about 2 a.m. when I arrived in Toronto. Finally I felt exhausted and wanted to sleep. I was running out of gas. Foolishly I failed to pull off the freeway sooner. I was still going through these freeway systems that had those two lanes veering to the right and left all the time. I prayed for God to help me as I watched the needle go below the E for empty and I saw myself off on the median, as an illegal alien. I also wasn't sure how much money I had left in my account. I was not keeping track.

I had been awake for too many hours, had not had a meal since the bacon in Milwaukee. I was terrified of the consequences. I was just too tired and needed gas.

Be of good courage, and let us be strong for our people and for the cities of our God.
And may the Lord do what is good in His sight.
2 Samuel 10:12

I had no choice, I had to exit, not seeing any signs of life. I was praying that God would save me. When I exited the freeway, I looked to the right, it was desolate.

My heart skipped a beat, was I going to run out of gas in the middle of nowhere? Then, I turned my head to the left and saw a 14-story hotel, a chain I recognized, was gleaming nearby. A gas station was a few hundred feet beyond it. When

I entered the hotel and got a room, it was mentioned to me that it takes five days for charges to show up on my debit card. I asked for five nights and went to sleep.

I slept eight hours and ate breakfast the next morning. I watched television, I rested, I ordered food. The next night I thought for sure that my friends were driving or flying out to meet me, a thought that came from absolutely nowhere. So, I went to the hotel dining room and ordered four meals that cost me $175. No one arrived to join me.

I stayed in the hotel for three days, really struggling with my pain. I had thrown my medicine, my pot, out the window of the car while I was driving due to my extreme paranoia. I was wishing in my hotel room that I had not been so impulsive. I was enduring extreme furnace pain throughout my body. The neuropathy that resulted from my 2004 brain surgery attacks all my weaknesses. The burning was in my legs, bottom of the feet, my groin from two past hernia surgeries, chest area from botched concave chest surgery, throat area from time I had a trachea, and of course the right side of my head where they opened it to do brain surgery. I was on fire and had not dealt with this before.

I was told in the biblical story in Daniel 3:14-29 that God saved Shadrach, Meshach and Abednego from the burning fiery furnace that King Nebuchadnezzar cast them into for expressing their loyalty to God. I prayed for God to deliver me from my furnace.

"Look!" he answered, "I see four men loose, walking in the midst of the fire; and they are not hurt, and the form of the fourth is like the Son of God."
Daniel 3:25

A Healing Cab Ride

My dad told me that a friend of mine was flying out that night with my birth certificate and to drive me back to Milwaukee. I knew she was coming in the evening so that morning I hired a taxi to drive me to a pharmacy or a clinic to get some help for my pain. I did not want to drive those freeways any more. All I could get was Tylenol at the pharmacy and the clinic wanted $130 cash for the appointment. I decided that was too much, so I told the cab driver to take me on a sight-seeing adventure. The cab driver looked in my eyes as I came up to the cab and saw that I was in pain. He told me that he had major surgery a few years back on his shoulder and he knew pain. Sitting in the front seat with the driver, I took off my socks and put my feet on the dashboard. He saw the discoloration of my neuropathy. My feet are red, purple, and black from lack of circulation. He cried.

I then put my hand on his shoulder. He asked, "Who are you?" I said, "I'm a servant of God." He said, "John, I don't feel any more pain in my shoulder." That three-hour ride cost me close to $300. That night he sent a friend who knew someone. We went and bought pot. The ride and the purchase cost another $200. I discovered I was out of money that night. I stopped at the hotel's ATM and was not able to get cash.

God Sends An Angel / A Friend to My Rescue

My friend from Milwaukee arrived at 11pm. I met her and we ate in the room. We had the leftover meals from the night before. I got high to relieve my neuropathy pain. All I needed was a few puffs. I became relaxed as the pain lessened. We opened an 1856 bottle of iced champagne I had from earlier. The year was 100 years before I was born. Note that there is meaningless meaning in little things when one is manic. I was drinking again because I was still not taking my medications, as if that's a sane justification.

The friend that came to get me was a very good friend, she had seen me through many operations and recoveries. She came because she was the only person that my ex-wife knew with a passport and the ability to handle me while manic. I don't get along with a lot of people when I'm manic. I really piss people off and they can't handle it, including my family.

24

My friend had a lot of courage to fly on a moment's notice, leave her family, her business, and her husband to hope to convince me to return with her. She did a lot of talking to get me to leave with her. We talked almost constantly through the night on our phones, she in her room, me in mine. She had a strategy to keep me up talking to grow me tired, so I would agree to return to Milwaukee. It worked. We left the hotel at 4 a.m. How she stayed awake to drive me home, I don't know. I do know that God was watching over us every step of the way.

For I, the Lord your God, will hold your right hand,
Saying to you, "Fear not, I will help you."
Isaiah 41:13

The Wacky Ride Home

When we left we had both been up more than 20 hours. We first went to a gas station since my tank was still on empty. I went inside and looked at post cards on a rack. I thought I would buy five, then it became ten. I kept looking and decided to buy all the post cards on the rack, I emptied the rack and put them all on the counter for the cashier. By this time, a line of people had formed behind me, the attendant said, "How many cards are there?" I replied, "I sure don't know." I started to count and said, "I'll buy ten."

The weather got bad, horrible rain storms, there was a lot of lightening across the sky. The weather slowed us down and also made us tired. While we were driving, she turned to me and said, "you really stink." I told her, "No the car seat stinks from what happened in Indiana when I had diarrhea." She sent a text to my ex-wife and family members for a rescue. It had become clear that she could not stay awake for the long trip. Certainly I could not trust me to drive and stay on course.

My two nephews helped by meeting us in Indiana. My nephews got quite an education in manic behavior when they had to deal with me one on one and try to drive at the same time. I felt bad for months that they had to see me that way. We arrived at another psych hospital at 8:30 p.m. My entire family and my ex-wife were there, quite an effort was made to make sure I was hospitalized that night. I am sure they all were exhausted from the numerous failed attempts to help me. After talking with the intake worker, I was let go. I was told to take aspirin if I was not going to take my blood thinner medication. After fully admitting that I was not taking any of my medications, they thought it somehow made sense to send me home. Again, I needed someone with some guts to tie me down.

Recovery Time?

My nephew drove me home after the family's failure to get me admitted. My dad instructed my nephew to disengage the fuel pump in my car once we returned from the hospital. I thought my nephew was going to spend the night with me, but he stayed just long enough for me to fall asleep. Before he left, he indeed tampered with my car so that I could not go anywhere. It was weird in the morning when he was not there, I wanted someone to be there with me. The family can't handle me, they abandon me as quickly as possible and don't understand how much I need them.

My pet rabbits were not at home either, my ex-wife had them. I was looking for someone or something comforting and it was not to be found. I went to look in the refrigerator and it was mostly bare. What a life I led, such disarray. I had a few cigarettes left, so I went out on my patio to sit down in the fresh air.

I reflected on how unbelievable the events were that had happened. How ridiculous it was, ending up in Toronto after a simple jaunt to Chicago. I could not figure out what happened to me. Why was I doing these things? What was going on? I grabbed my Bible, read soothing scriptures and prayed. The sun on my face and the verses game me comfort.

Let everything that has breath praise the Lord!
Praise the Lord!
Psalm 150:6

How fitting that I would read that from Psalm 150:6 scripture, to praise the Lord, as my life was once again in shambles. The pain that was not at all in my mind was getting even worse as I started to come down from the manic, I could feel the depression coming on in my thoughts. My income was stolen away from me weeks earlier. I suspected that it was one of my employees who stole the company van with all the equipment in it. What was I going to do? How was I going to take care of myself? No income, no car, extreme pain, no reason to live.

I had been restless during the night with extreme pain that was now keeping me awake. I was being kept awake like torture now that I was finally tired enough and non-manic enough to want to sleep. When morning finally came, I sat out in the sun in my backyard and felt as if I was in a furnace burning up. I could barely drag myself back into the apartment.

I called my ex-wife, I was wondering if she would reject me. She was in the middle of a day at her counseling internship site. She heard the desperation and pain in my voice. She came immediately and helped me get my act together. She forced me to take some Tylenol so that I could function to get in the car and endure the wait at a clinic. We went to a local urgent care clinic. It was the only place she could think of that I had not been to in the recent months for medical attention with my pain.

When we arrived there, I could not get out of the car, the pain in my legs was so burning like an inferno, that I was now crying. I got into a wheelchair that was outside in the parking lot. We waited awhile, but the doctor who saw me was the answer to prayer, finally. She had such a compassionate bedside manner and treated me like a person in pain, not like a mental patient.

We talked about my mental illness and the fact that I had not been taking care of myself or taking my medications. She did not judge, she told me how sorry she was that I carried bipolar illness through life as she felt that it was the cancer of the mental illnesses.

After a short medical history, she quickly ordered an ultra sound of my legs. Ah, someone who gets it!! They rushed me into the room with the equipment. The technician did what I am certain they are told not to do. She told me that I was likely going to die any minute from the amount of blood clots in my legs, and that she had to leave the room to go find the doctor.

The doctor said that realistically, I was not in a condition that warranted a hospital stay, and since it was the start of the Memorial Day holiday weekend, she would order that I get Lovenox shots daily for five days. I could resolve the medication situation by taking my meds and then seeing my hematologist and primary doctor to get back on track. Since I was required to stay with someone due to my fragile state, I went home with my ex-wife and slept for a couple of weeks while my body and my mind healed as much as was possible.

... Fear not, for I have redeemed you;
I have called you by your name;
You are Mine.
Isaiah 43:1

Chapter 3: A Musician's High and Low Notes

Make haste, O God, to deliver me!
Make haste to help me, O Lord.
Psalm 70:1

UWM – Almost Success

I drove a nice car, wore nice clothes and was taking classes at the University of Wisconsin Milwaukee. I was 22 years old. Soon my behavior was going to change. As I neared the spring, another manic swing came on. At the time, I did not know what was happening to me. I would just either feel hopeless, or I had more energy than I knew what to do with. Even the psychiatrists I saw did not educate me about what was happening. I just recently learned that the seasons of the mind flow often with the seasons of the weather.

Coming into each spring, I was in my mind and body, dead and depleted. Then just like snapping a twig, I felt great. The sun was shining again.

While attending UWM, I worked. I worked at a carpet cleaning plant putting area rugs into the cleaning machine. I worked harder than ever before. It was fun, I was having a ball, everything is a blast when I am manic. I had been there for a year while I was going to school. Now that I was manic, no longer depressed, my classes were no longer difficult to understand. I was on the fast track of mania, still without medication.

At the university, I became director of the jazz ensemble for UWM basketball games. This was a dream come true, to direct this group who performed during halftime and time-outs. I had been studying to be a music educator. Directing a band was something I enjoyed doing. This was my time to prove myself and shine. Since my brain was on manic overdrive, I got in a yelling match with the Athletic Director and got thrown out of a game.

New Orleans Troubles

In my impulsive, irrational, screwed up mind -- that night I took my car, my trombone, and one suitcase of clothes and left town. I drove to Dallas, Texas to see my brother and his wife. I also impulsively decided to quit school and my job. I had just enough money to get to Dallas.

After I arrived, I sold my car to my brother. I needed the money to buy a round trip ticket for a flight to New Orleans. I had gone to New Orleans to find a way to play my music there. I was out of school and out of a job, a new place to start over. The airline lost my suitcase and my trombone. I ended up in the French Quarter sitting and drinking cognac until the wee hours of the morning. I was picked up by a pimp at around 4 am. He waited patiently as we spent two hours trying to cash my traveler's checks. After I had the cash, I ended up in a seedy hotel deep in the inner part of the city with a woman.

I remember being concerned that when we got to the hotel, I noticed there was no lock on the door. I took off the Stetson hat that I was wearing. I dropped down on the bed and fell asleep. God protected me, I am so grateful that I fell asleep. The next morning I came out of the hotel to find a group of about ten men at the curb. They said, "honkey, you are on the wrong side of the street." I asked if they could just show me how I could get back to the YMCA. They showed me and did not fight me. I told them I was a jazz musician that got turned around. They all laughed, "Yeah you got turned around."

I made it to the YMCA for an overnight stay, then flew back to my brother's house. When I arrived back at the airport, I was able reclaim my trombone and luggage that they had lost. On the trip home, the flight attendant told me she needed to put my trombone in the front closet. I told her, "No this trombone is my lover, and she is more exciting than any woman I have met." She let me keep my trombone sitting next to me.

My Adventure in the 17-foot RV

My bipolar illness had six-month swings almost to the day during my 20's. I was playing my trombone a few hours every day, I was excited again. I thought that my life was falling back together. In my excitement, I called up my jazz trombone teacher in Chicago, Illinois. He had a great idea for me. He set up an audition for me at a prominent music school, Eastman School of Music in Rochester, New York.

I needed a way to get there. Since I sold my car to my brother, I did not have a car. My dad took me to one of those places where you can drive the car to a destination, pay for the gas and they give you $100 when you deliver the car. We found a company that would let me drive a car to Rochester.

While I was there with dad, I saw that they had some RV's on the lot. They were deluxe models, the interiors were all decked out. I said, "I want to buy one of these, much more fun to drive to Rochester in." Recall, I was very elevated manic, therefore impulsive and irrational. I did not have money to buy this RV. I acted like I did, but I was nearly broke. Somehow I convinced the owner that I needed to test drive the RV for 24 hours and then I would be back with the money.

Later that day I showed up at my parent's house with the RV. I convinced dad that I was buying the RV. I went in the house, brought out some clothes and a stereo. Off I went to a friend's house, picked up three friends and declared, "Let's go to Chicago to party." We stopped to buy some alcohol. I pulled into a parking structure to wait. Upon leaving, I failed to read the height of the parking structure. Consequently, as I drove, the air conditioning units on top of the RV tore off.

We continued on to Chicago, stopping at a gas station to stuff inner tubes of tires into the holes where the air conditioning units were. Early the next morning we returned and I dropped off my friends. This wasn't the end of the adventure. I still had plenty of irrational thoughts and impulsive actions coming on. I decided to drive to Rochester, New York. Remember – that was my original destination with a loaner car.

When I hit Escanaba, Michigan I started to have electrical problems and then the crankshaft fell off, stopping me in my tracks. I called the RV dealer and told him what happened. When I told him that I would settle up with him after I got back from my audition, he was furious. I had to leave the vehicle by the side of the road. Of course it was my magic number of $4000 that it cost me to resolve it with the dealer who had to have it towed from Escanaba and repaired.

I always thought that God was responsible for the crankshaft falling off, he protected me from ending up in jail in Canada for vehicle theft.

Seek the Lord while He may be found,
Call upon Him while he is near.
Isaiah 55:6

Eastman School of Music
After abandoning the RV, I still had my destination in mind. It was winter. I put on my ski bibs, winter coat, hat and gloves that I had put into the RV. I grabbed my trombone case, my music case, and started walking to the Canada border. When I got there I had some explaining to do because I didn't have a passport or luggage. All I had were my irrational thoughts. The immigration official asked me how I was going to get to Rochester. I showed them a map of the hitchhike route I had planned. They let me in.

I remember getting very tired from walking in the cold; truckers had given me rides here and there. It was a clear sky, thousands of stars and a bright moon; almost felt like the sun was out. It became very late and bitter cold. It began to snow, and quickly became a blizzard. For the first time on the trip I felt afraid. My only choice was to keep walking on the side of the freeway. I started to pray for help, to be picked up, to get warm. I prayed for some way to get over the border back in the

United States. Suddenly I saw the taillights of a car pull ahead of me and stop. The driver was an elderly woman who rolled down her window and asked, "Do you need a ride?"

I climbed in the front seat. I put my music case and trombone in the back seat. I thanked her and thanked her for stopping. She said, "I almost missed you." I was grateful that she saw me in the thick snow. We were an hour from the U.S. border, so I could relax, get warm, and feel safe for awhile. I told her I had been hitchhiking. She asked, "Do you have papers?" I told her I did not. She confidently replied, "Don't worry, I will get you across."

God intervened again and allowed me safe travel with her. When we reached the border, she told me to fake that I was sleeping. I don't know how, but it worked. She got me back into the U.S. and took me all the way to my destination, Rochester. Answer to my prayer? Yes it was. Many bad things could have happened, yet God directed my path. To me the whole experience was very spiritual, trusting God to keep me safe. He not only kept me safe. That sweet angel from God drove me right to Eastman School of Music, and in time for my audition.

My Audition, Another Brush with Success

I met the trombone Professor John Marcellus the night before my formal audition. He asked me to prepare a trombone duet for the morning lesson. He gave me some staff paper and said, "Good luck!"

I found a room with a piano. I sat down and came up with the type of song I like. It was a simple melody with pretty harmony. In the morning for my audition, I gave my composition to the Professor. He was very impressed said I had the ability to write. What I wrote reminded him of a Christian ballad he liked. He showed me the music and it was similar, I remember it had touching lyrics. He told me he would very much like to teach me further but he said, "Come here to do your master's work when you finish your undergrad degree."

Dead end! I thought this audition would get me into a school where I could be motivated somehow to complete my bachelor's degree there. I knew I would never be able to finish my degree in Milwaukee. I had tried three times; two during mania and once when I was suicidal. I had to drop out three times, it was impossible to think or study and the manic swings led to arguments with my professors.

Here I was, I passed an audition at one of the most prestigious music schools in the country, but that master's degree opportunity would never come. Funny thing, I actually failed my audition three years earlier at UWM. They only took me because my tuition had already been paid and my mother was in the master's program for music therapy at the time. Was it manic energy or manic creativity that day at Eastman? Sadly, soon after that audition I slipped into a deep depression season again.

My Naked Weekend in Jail

I got an idea when I was 24 years old in when I was back in a manic swing to put a big band together I called my jazz teacher in Chicago and he referred me to his friend in Indiana who had jazz charts for a big band as I was trying to put together a jazz big band, and the charts were for free.

I remember back then, that I owned a van, and I was ready to go a full tank of gas and $13.00 in my pocket. So I went home, filled the van with my music, belongings, and some clothes, and off I went. I said, "Jesus will help me with my gas issue. Now, I had my boom box worth $300.00 with me, and when I had used up my gas money I stopped at a weigh station and sold it to a sheriff for $10.00 enough to get me to where I was going or so I thought.

I was outside of Rockford, Illinois, when I ran out of gas. A trucking company truck from Rockford, saw my van parked on the side of the road and determined that I needed to be pulled back into town to their shop. Once there, I called a family member to send some money, and he hung up the phone.

The company was closing, and I had no choice but to grab my trombone and head downtown until the morning. I would need to find some money and pay off the trucking company to get my van back. Wandering around, I was led to a street church in downtown Rockford. I was hoping for a meal and a place to stay, when I met two men, a pastor of a church and his friend. The conversation started out okay, but soon the subject turned to the trombone and they wanted to hear me play. I told them about my education and years of playing in jazz groups, when the pastor told me that he thought I was worshipping an idol.

The conversation became ugly and heated, so I opened up the trombone case and brought out the slide. In front of them, I bent the slide in two and gave it to them. I said, "Here is my idol." Never before had I ever damaged my trombones! They said that there was no place for me to stay overnight, nor would they share a meal. I left in more trouble than I had come in with. I was in a strange town, no place to sleep, no money in my pockets. I was in trouble, and too prideful to contact family or friends.

I started to walk, not knowing where I was going. I ended up deep in the inner city. It was late and dark. I prayed for Jesus to help. Around midnight, I saw a group of people outside of a home. I walked up to them. It was poker night, and they were taking a break from playing. They invited me inside. I watched for a few hours, ate with them, and went to leave.

In front of the house, a man put a hand gun to my left temple. I did my best to talk him out of pulling the trigger. He did not want money, but just to kill a white boy. I scared him when I started to talk crazy about how Jesus would not let me die in front of him, that Jesus would torture him the rest of his life, and that he would beg for freedom. I told him it was just like hell where he was going throughout eternity. He hit me over the head and knocked me out. I awoke later and thanked God for saving my life.

Though I walk in the midst of trouble, You will revive me; You will stretch our Your hand against the wrath of my enemies, and Your right hand will save me.
Psalm 138:7

At sometime later. I picked myself up and off I went walking. In another few hours, I met a man who let me come into his home and sleep. I returned to the trucking company in the morning.

I did not have any money to pay the trucking company. The owner feared for my safety, so he had me arrested for vagrancy. Police pulled up and stuffed me into their vehicle. Once I arrived at the police station, they asked me for all my clothes, and then two cops roughed me up a bit. It was Friday night. Finally I got a meal, and I started to communicate to the cell next to me, through the food tray opening. This was not a cell with bars, but full enclosure. Being naked in a lit cell was not any fun and I wondered what I might have done differently.

On Saturday evening the police put another inmate in my cell. I was laying on my bunk when he came over to me, sat down, and put his hand on my upper thigh. He said, "You have a nice nest." I removed his hand and said it would be a war if he tried anything, because I was not interested. It was impossible to fall asleep because he was constantly on me. Eventually I asked him why he was in jail.

He told me, years earlier he was arrested for armed robbery and when he arrived at the Joliet, Illinois prison he was put in a cell with a large man who told him he had one of two options. One be sodomized and perform oral sex, or be beaten up every day. He chose to be beaten up every day, until he was unable to defend himself any longer, so he gave in, and felt for five years he was a homosexual. When he got out of prison he accepted a job at a restaurant where the same thing happened. The restaurant owner paid him $50,000.00 a year for sexual favors and the way he dealt with it was to get drunk on the weekends and end up in jail.

I told him he now had a new choice: quit his job and stay away from people that wanted to harm him in this way. I told him to trust himself and attempt to change his life. I have always been a good listener with people telling me their life stories even when I was manic and ill. Monday morning I was put in a room with everyone who was going to see the judge. Most of them wore orange jump suits. The stories began, each person telling why he was in jail. To my left were maybe 10 people. The first one said he got in an argument with his wife, picked up a knife and stabbed her to death. Wow! I was sitting there! Another said he was hungry and smashed a Sentry window to grab some bread, but tried to get money from the till, so it was armed robbery. Another stole a car. My cellmate became drunk and destroyed property. When it came to my time, I said I was a jazz musician that ran out of money.

When it was my turn to see the judge, I was afraid of what might happen, so I pleaded guilty. The judge said I served my sentence and I was free to go. My dad and my pastor and brother came down to pick me up. Dad paid the trucking company to get my van back.

Finally, Rubbing Elbows With Musicians

I had a manic itch to return to New York City. I had referrals this time, for a job and a place to stay. I was 23 years old. I took $200 with me and did not worry. I trusted that if this was where God wanted me to be, everything would work out. I drove a car to Queens and dropped it off for a fee of $100, no adventures in the car this time.

I ended up at the YMCA next to Central Park. I was not able to reach my lodging contact through our church. I took the subway to the publishing company where I had a referral to for a job interview. I talked with the son of the owner at Charles Colin Publishing since the owner was not in. We had a nice conversation but nothing came from the visit.

I read in the *Village Voice* newspaper that trombonist Slide Hampton was playing at Village Vanguard jazz club. I went down to the club to hear Slide play with tenor saxophonist Dexter Gordon. I listened to them play a very exhilarating first set. I walked up to Slide at the break. I introduced myself and asked if he would be playing blues in the next set. They knocked out the house with their playing that night. There was an instant connection between us. That night we talked and he offered to help me.

Slide was a protégé of J.J. Johnson. I had played along with J.J. Johnson records for years and loved the style. This felt too good to be true, but for years we would have wonderful phone conversations after I left New York. Slide was different from the jazz musicians I knew. He was a vegetarian and he did not do drugs or drink alcohol.

That night at Village Vanguard I asked Slide if I could audition for him. He said yes and told me to meet him at Charles Colin Publishing where he had a studio. Was it coincidence, or God's orchestration of events?

The next morning I went to the publishing company, this time the father Charles was there. Slide had not come in yet, so I spoke to Charles. I explained that a French horn professor at my university had referred me. We talked back and forth until he asked me if I was looking for a job. I said yes. He said it was a salesman job at a music store in Times Square. Just as I opened my lips to say yes, Slide Hampton poked his head in to say hi. It was wonderful the way the whole thing unfolded. Before I could think about what was happening, Slide Hampton was walking me over to Giardinelli's for my interview. On the way, we stopped off and Slide took me to lunch. It was a nice informal way to talk with him and get to know him.

I got the job at Giardinelli's on the second day I was in New York City. On my first day of work, jazz trumpeter Dizzy Gillespie came in the store and walked up to me at the counter. He was there to get his valve repaired, I admired the unusually shaped bell on his trumpet. Man, I was on top of the world! Working all day and talking with musicians was outstanding. Unfortunately, I was quickly running out of cash. The church had still not come through with lodging arrangements.

The next day I told the owner of the music store that I had to quit my job. I was running out of money, I was earning $4 an hour, not enough to cover my $30 a night stay at the YMCA. It was the hardest decision I have ever made. That night at the YMCA, the woman from the church called. She apologized for taking so long to get back to me and told me they had a room for me. I told her I had quit my job and was down to pennies. I thanked her for calling but I did not have enough faith to stay and work it out with Giardinelli's.

I was in my sixth month of the mania, meaning I was coming down, therefore deep dark depression was on the horizon. Next, I phoned a woman in Milwaukee who I had been dating. She sent me a train ticket to come back home.

Six Months Later, Mania Means Music -- Again

The next year in the spring, I swung back into the manic side of my illness like clockwork. I decided to bring Slide Hampton to Milwaukee for a concert. He had never played in Milwaukee before. I sold one of my trombones for four Stan Kenton music arrangements that required five trombones, one flute, and 25 strings. I hired all those musicians. Twenty-five string players came from the Milwaukee Symphony Orchestra. I put the concert together in three weeks (typical manic behavior, everything always in a rush). More of that manic 'luck' surrounded me – I was able to get a write-up in the local newspaper and free promos on radio stations.

The four Stan Kenton charts were played in the first set. The second set was Slide, myself plus violin, guitar, conga, drums, piano and bass. Slide played a beautiful tribute to his friend Thelonious Monk, a tremendous jazz pianist and composer who had just passed away. I held my own pretty well for not having practiced for six months. I don't play my horn when I am in the season of suicidal despair. Everyone that came that night enjoyed themselves.

On the business side of things, the day before the concert, dad asked me how many tickets I had sold. I had sold only 100, and needed to sell 600 tickets to break even. I was manic and all over the place in my mind and my actions, but not focused on how to pay the musicians and other costs. Mania does many things, at times makes you very stupid. I wanted the musicians and music to be perfect, that was all I knew.

Dad took me to the bank, cosigned a loan for $4000. That $4000 had to be turned over to the musician's union president before the concert at the doorway. I was not in the union but everyone else was. I can't imagine what might have happened if I showed up without that money. My dad came to my aid, securing cosigned loans numerous times over the years. Most manic episodes include spending large sums of money that I do not have.

And the pressure was off. End result: After expenses, I lost $4000, but the jazz music and musicians were top notch. Slide told me that if I had spent more time on the concert, it would have been a financial success. In my mind, the music and the event itself was a great success, but I did not celebrate afterwards with musicians, friends, family. No, I was manic. After the concert, I needed to be harnessed down, but off I went. I drove down to Illinois with the $500 I had earned from the concert. I stopped at a strip club, and had a two-hour massage.

And forgive us our sins, for we also forgive everyone who is indebted to us.
And do not lead us into temptation, but deliver us from the evil one.
Luke 11:4

Chapter 4: Childhood Memories & Signs of Trouble

Train a child in the way he should go,
and when he is old he will not turn from it.
Proverbs 22:6

My Life Before Bipolar and Addictions

It is commonly said, "God does not make junk." Whether this was created for a bumper sticker or is words of wisdom from a theologian is not known. In spite of all that has happened to me, I am able to respect God's power and ability to make me so complex that I love deeply, I have run businesses, I have healed. God is able to pull me deeper and deeper into an understanding of how to live my life by surrendering to Him each day, to understand his reward of peace.

It took most of my adult life for me to fully understand God's grace and boundaries as good Fatherly guidance. My mental and physical illnesses tested my ability to surrender to God whether as a young boy or grown man. My life, filled with severe physical and mental hardships, has given me the opportunity to build a meaningful relationship with the Lord and others. My focus and comfort with my faith started with the strong Christian upbringing in my family.

I was born in Milwaukee, Wisconsin. I am the third child of four. I grew up with an older brother who became an architect with my dad; an older sister who danced and now runs a dance company. My younger sister danced on a scholarship in classes at the Joffrey Ballet, and went on to dance professionally. She is now an awesome mom to four girls. We are close in age, all in our 50's at this time. My brother died four years ago when he was 54. My mom joined him in heaven in November 2011. We miss them both.

My father has been a dedicated architect, working until he was 82. Our childhood was spent working and playing on our small ten-acre farm in Brookfield, a suburb of Milwaukee. Mom was always preparing food, playing the piano, working in the garden. She had gifts that would carry her throughout her life. She later was in college with me at the same time, getting her master's degree in music therapy while I was studying to be a band leader and music teacher.

We had farm equipment. I remember a tractor, a wagon, a cutter and a baler. We baled our own hay because we needed the hay to feed our 4 horses. I remember it was hard work baling the hay. Sometimes the baler would leave bales on the ground and we would have to throw the bales up on the wagon while another person would stack the bales on the wagon. The most fun was stacking the bales in the barn.

My older brother and I had great fun with the neighborhood kids on our small hobby farm. I have memories of stacking hay in the barn, then we would swing down from the rafters into the hay. My brother built tree houses and one was in the rafters of the barn. We climbed up a ladder then across on a beam to get to it. When a quick exit was in order, we could just fall into the hay below. This was something all of us enjoyed over and over.

In the morning before school one of us would go up to the barn and throw down the hay from the second floor for the horses to eat. Then to fill up their water container, and finally, to make sure they had their salt bar and feed.

Within the group of horses, our mare Subi was the boss, always biting the hind-quarters of the other mares to keep them in line. These are special fond memories that I have never forgotten.

One time when I was about nine years old, my dad and I were out with the horses, riding in an open field. When we decided to head a different direction, and my horse slipped on ice and went down. Somehow I removed my foot from the stirrup and stayed away from danger. I know God did it for me, it happened too quickly for me to have consciously gotten out of harm's way. I could have easily broken a leg or worse with the weight of the horse. I jumped up, got back on the horse and we continued our journey. My life has been much like that, slipping and crashing -- to have God pick me up so that I can move on.

Be pleased, O Lord to deliver me;
O Lord, make haste to help me.
Psalm 40:13

Christian Thinking, Christian Values
      What did it mean to grow up in a Christian home? I remember when I was six or seven years old I was having a discussion with dad about what Christmas was all about. I grinned ear to ear and said, " Early Christmas morning we wake up and go downstairs to see what Santa gave us, then see if he ate the food we left for him." Dad sternly looked at me and said, "John that is important but what about your friend Jesus Christ? He was born today. We are going to celebrate his birthday." I was humbled that day by the Holy Spirit through my father's wise simple words. Sure, I was attending church every Sunday, but after that Christmas day I would never forget who Jesus was.

The righteous man walks in his integrity;
his children are blessed after him.
Proverbs 20:7

      The mind thinks clearest when Jesus is directing the day. I have finally learned this lesson. I have always been called a late bloomer, and at times the prodigal son. I am 55 and I finally get it, I must keep God and Jesus the main focus of my thinking and my life, then and I am at peace. Free of addictions, I am much like a kid again, carefree, full of hope for the future.

I Can't Do Simple Things

We lived in a three-bedroom farmhouse. My brother and I shared a room, and my two sisters shared another. The rooms were tiny, we had trundle beds, where you pull out the bed from underneath and pull it up. Not much room, but we did have a desk that went from wall to wall for school work and projects.

My brother sat at that desk and assembled model fighter jets, many of them. He would carefully glue the pieces together and then add the decals. I was only able to watch him put these planes together, I could not do it. When I got up the confidence to try to put one together, it was the most difficult thing I had ever tried at the time. I failed miserably. I felt so inferior, seeing him do it so easily. My brother continued until he filled the whole ceiling with these planes.

Just a few years ago, in the process of some medical testing, I was diagnosed with Klinefelter Syndrome. It is a learning disability of sorts and explained a lot of things that I have never been able to do. I remember when the family was in Europe on my dad's fellowship there, when I was two years old. We were pointing at the many pigeons in the square. I was unable to speak words until I was four. When I looked at the pigeons, I called them "ga ga". It has always been extremely difficult for me to put anything together with my hands, and I cannot read instructions and understand either.

We also had a racetrack in the basement. Of course I never won when I raced against my brother, but with neighbor friends, I fared better. On a given afternoon, five or six friends would be competing. My brother would eventually say to me, "Lets' race." and he would start out slowly, then catch up to me. All of a sudden I would get excited and push full throttle and spin out or crash and he would win. My brother's nickname was fast Eddie, he raced BMW's in a BMW club. He had an edge with me, my mental illness frustrated him I think. The only thing I could beat him at was pool or ping-pong which we played only a few times.

My brother died in November 2008, from a massive heart attack. In the months before he died, he reached out and seemed to want to have a relationship, he offered that I could stay with him if needed when my divorce was finalized in 2009. He was the brother I always wanted but did not have.

Our hay field to the north of our farm land was perfect for a race track. I learned how to drive stick shift on my dad's VW Gia Convertible. My brother and I would take mom and dad's cars up in the hay field. We would beat them up, go around in an oval like they were off road vehicles. Dad had an aerial photo taken of the farm, and the picture showed a race track ring in the hay field. That's how he found out that we were driving the cars in the field.

Boy Scouts

My dad was an Eagle Scout so I wanted to reach that too. The goal was to accomplish tasks and then receive a merit badge. I have many fond memories camping in the summer, getting my canoeing merit badge. I remember the coolest thing to do was swamping a canoe by flooding it with water and seeing that it will not sink. If you turn the canoe over and swim under it, there is an air pocket to breathe from.

When we camped in the winter we boiled snow for drinking water. It was difficult to be a Boy Scout camping in the middle of winter. Boy Scouts was fun learning so many things that were useful in life. It felt good for me to be able to accomplish things, it was easier when someone showed me how to do things.

As you can see, I like to think about childhood memories of the fun and carefree days, when mental illness had not yet invaded my brain and my life.

While I live I will praise the Lord; I will sing
praises to my God while I have my being.
Psalm 146:2

Smooth Sailing

There were things I tried just because my brother or dad did it, and I learned by doing. Dad had a pilot's license for small planes and he would fly for business purposes. Once in a while he would take us kids along. Sometimes I would get to fly alone with him. It did not matter if dad was flying small planes or sailing his 28- foot sailboat. His enjoyment came when the weather would get bad, actually extremely high winds and storms were his favorite, he liked a challenge. I learned from him not to fear, just learn how to do it right. Sailing dad's boat for many years was something I excelled at until my brain aneurysm.

I always enjoyed times alone with dad, and time on the boat was one of those rare opportunities. Even as a kid, would show me how and let me fly the plane too. I learned from him that being too small was not a limitation. He showed me how to use the instruments and fly the plane just fine. Repetition was the key for me in learning something. If someone showed me, I learned, and my self-confidence soared.

Dad was no slouch when it came to safety, it was important. When I was about 40, he said, "If you want to sail my sailboat on Lake Michigan, you have to pass the Coast Guard Auxiliary test." The Coast Guard Auxiliary offered classes and were enjoyable. I was nervous because I knew it was hard for me to study things in a book and comprehend it. But I am not one to go down easily, so I agreed to take the test. When it came time to tie different knots, I tied all of them except the bow line. The instructor looked at me and said "John you have done a great job of learning the information, I am not going to hold you back for not being able to tie the bow line."

I showed dad my certificate and patch, and he allowed me to sail his boat out on Lake Michigan. His 28-foot sailboat became an evening regular occurrence during the week, with co-workers and friends of mine. Finally, something I was not afraid of that I could do well. There were bad weather times when I handled the boat well. I was also able to teach passengers how to help crew the boat when we were out, it was fun.

I never sailed that boat when I was manic, what a blessing that is. God protected me from harm again, I can't imagine what the bad judgment and impulsive actions of mania may have done with me at the control of a boat.

And if anyone thinks that he knows anything,
he knows nothing yet as he ought to know
But if anyone loves God, this one is known by Him.
1 Corinthians 8:2-3

Teenage Exploration – Time for Addictions

When our family moved from the rural farm to the east side of Milwaukee, into the city life, something dreadful began. Temptation was everywhere, and I was ripe for it! First, my new friends had porn magazines- something to look at and not easy to put away. I kept many in a stack in my room. I would put Penthouse inside my schoolbook and look at them during class in high school. My addictions took hold and soared. The porn fed into masturbation, too much masturbation. I know that teenagers have a high sex drive, but it consumed me such that I could not concentrate on much else. Then I was introduced to pot, it relaxed me. I could not stop my new addictions, to me they were fun. I could not see their destructive nature at that age. Sexual thoughts were constant. I was being consumed by addictions.

Where was Jesus? Satan had me curious and held me captive. I was arrested my junior year for marijuana but because I was a minor there is no record. Did it stop my smoking? No it did not. It was a daily vice. I was consumed in a fire that I was quite comfortable in.

I went out for my high school tennis team. I had never played before. In my second year of playing, my senior year, I was on a doubles team that placed in the city finals. I earned a varsity letter in a sport I had not played prior. Every day, before I walked to the tennis court for practice, I stopped at home and smoked a small pipe of hash. I wonder how good I would have been if I wasn't high all the time.

The addiction had me trapped, with the exception of swim team season. I was on the swim team all four years of high school. I did not smoke hash or pot when swimming five afternoons a week. I have a concave chest that brought strange looks from other swimmers, I looked different. My upper chest went in where it was supposed to look raised. Not easy in those years. Being a teenager with a deformed looking chest isn't fun, but God made me like this so can't say or do much about it. Swimming was great for my lungs.

Time to Pick up My Horn

I played trombone in school bands. Strangely, I was never taught how to read music. During lessons, the band director would teach me how to play the song by rote, so that was how I did it. It was quite silly. Why was I not taught how to read music?

I decided to attend college. I was very insecure, but I had a new start. I decided to follow in the footsteps of my mother. She was already studying for her master's degree in music therapy. When I auditioned on my trombone for the music education degree program, the trombone professor was shocked when he heard me play. I could not read a note on the sheet music. He went to the head of the music committee and said, "I can't teach this student; he does not know how to read music." He was told to teach me because I had paid the tuition and was in the program. They put me on probation in the music history program for a year to see what would happen by the end of the year.

This is where Jesus came in. He controls our future. My professor is a symphony orchestra trombonist, a professional on a high level. He played for our local symphony orchestra for almost 40 years as principal trombonist. He gave me a lesson once a week for three years. I met with him later in my life for lessons for thirty years. He is a disciple of the trombone; he did so much for my career as a player. He taught me the foundation of the instrument. Yes, he taught me about time and how to read the notes correctly, and about how to breathe. He taught me to have a sweet tone.

He is a Godly Christian man who has been a lifelong friend and mentor, accepting me as I am with my ups and downs. He also sat with my wife in the waiting room all day during one of my surgeries, such a blessing. He has a calming and giving spirit. I am grateful to know him.

What is most important is our friendship. Now that it is 30 years later, he and I call each from time to time and share scripture verses with each other. That first semester in college, I played last chair in the lowest level band. It was a start, a foundation to build on. He lit a fire in me and soon I was practicing four to five hours a day. The next semester, probation was lifted, I was put back into the music education program.

Praise the Lord!
For it is good to sing praises to our God;
for it is pleasant, and praise is beautiful.
Psalm 147:1

I always appreciated my classical roots as taught at the university, but jazz was more my style. During my second year at UWM, I also took a class at the Wisconsin Conservatory of Music when I heard about the professor's reputation as a jazz instructor. Miles Davis, J.J. Johnson and Slide Hampton were my favorites, I played along with their music. I changed my focus and decided that I was not going to be a teacher. I wanted to be a professional jazz trombonist.

My life felt together for the first time and I was happy. That summer I went on a two-week tour of Europe, playing with fifty or so members of our university ensemble. A rare window of success for me, life was sweet. However, I feared how I would do the core classes. I had a comprehension problem and in a way I protected myself by taking mostly music courses. I passed math and english, only by taking each twice. I was busy learning how to play different instruments.

I was turned on with composition and arrangement classes. Anything that was creative interested me. I passed a music history exam but I memorized material for two days straight. I didn't know it, I only memorized it for the test. People told me I was doing well, but I was becoming more and more afraid. My trombone playing was at an all time high, but my mind was crumbling. I did not know what to do about it, and then I collapsed into suicidal depression.

I knew who Jesus was and did my best to talk to him. Satan was stronger in my mind, and my mental illness was starting in on my brain. The next period of my life would include numerous attempts to finish college which my mental illness would not allow. My faith was not strong enough to fight the addictions, to get the help I needed, or even understand what was happening to me. I had no idea that my brain was sick, very sick indeed. I also had no idea that it was NOT my fault, and I did NOT cause it.

CHAPTER 5: Suicide is the Question, God is the Answer

*Oh, that I may have my request, that God would grant me
the thing that I long for!*
That it would please God to crush me, that
He would loose His hand and cut me off!
Job 6:8-9

Suicidal depression in my life occurred from age 20 through 35, at six-month intervals, rotating with six months of mania. The psychiatrist that I was seeing misdiagnosed my bipolar illness. He felt that I was just not adjusting to adulthood. He let me function in an insane manner for seven years without any medication. When he finally prescribed lithium, I went another seven years without the doctor checking for the therapeutic level of lithium. I was still a wreck in many ways and he didn't see it.

Suicide, or not suicide?

I so badly wanted to be normal at age 20, but then the swings down into the abyss put me into a deep suicidal wave of depression. I could not understand. Even though it happened year after year at the same time, it confused me every time. I was so powerless to do anything about it.

My mind could not grasp anything that was normal or made sense; everything was centered on planning my death. How could I be like this? I was raised in a loving Christian family, yet I am in an unfamiliar place. Where was God when I was in this despair? God was in me, keeping me safe from myself. I knew that Jesus suffered as a man; He knew the depth of my anguish.

Suicidal depression is like having no taste buds, no ability to plan the future and to look past the very second, as everything is internalized. The focus is working toward everything in the planning of my death. First, how was I going to complete suicide? When was I going to do it? Over and over again, like a scratched broken record, very annoying when it will not stop.

I had to have a good plan, one that did not just land me in the hospital. This was a fear for a long time, that I would stupidly not succeed and seriously harm myself and have to live with that. Guilt came as I thought of my family members whom I loved so much. As I planned my death each time, it was the loss of them and my loss to them that bothered me. Then came the panic attacks that had me in an anxiety-ridden fog that took away my ability to fathom reality. The panic attacks felt like a shark biting into me and tossing me back and forth, biting down harder and harder. I was losing all control of thoughts, like I was a programmed monster that was being controlled against my will by a horrible force at the control switch. At time the physical feeling was so overwhelming, it felt like I was being electrocuted.

Those close to me, such as family and friends, seem to like it when I am depressed, as I am quiet and out of the way in my darkness. They do not understand the severity of the emotional pain, weakness and confusion that suffocates my thinking and my ability to do simple things.

My experience with suicidal depression started when I entered my third year of college at 20 years of age. I felt like I was sliding down a wet mudslide, unable to grasp anything to keep from falling into a very deep hole. When I hit bottom I was unable to pull myself up on the sides. I kept falling downward even further at times when I thought I was already at the bottom. Very strange physical sensations that the mind creates.

One time I was lying on my bed with my Bible open across my chest, crying out to God to save me from the constant fear and panic. It's impossible to have peace when you feel the real terror of a tall building falling on top of you. You have no relief in it falling or in the thought going away, it just keeps falling at you. Panic attacks overwhelmed me and terrorized my mind, but God stood still. I was frustrated why he did not remove my pain. When I was a mess, I could not mentally rationalize that God was within me.

Unable To Take My Life

Suicide is a very touchy subject when it comes to mental illness. Destruction occurs in one's mind. The desire is to escape the constant panic attacks and hopeless thinking, and just end it, *JUST MAKE IT STOP!* Most often as in my case, family and friends were not able to identify with what I was enduring, such as planning my death, having no hope, or trying to catch my breath from the panic. I remember being totally consumed by fear on the inside but could hide it. I would participate in family events, but always knowing that next Tuesday I was taking my life. Always planning, but never taking my life.

I developed anger when I was suicidal. I was angry at myself, at life, at no solution. For 15 years every six months I experienced these suicidal trials. Every fall and winter when I became suicidal, I planned my death all darn day long, almost every day. The mind is so convinced that death is the only way out. The rejection of life becomes all-consuming because that is all you can see, you don't see or consider any other options. Such focused thinking that excludes all else has to be mental illness, it's just odd.

My terror multiplied because it became obvious that I was not capable of killing myself. I even failed at killing myself. I felt so defeated, not able to doing anything. I felt I was a failure, a coward.

There was another stressor I considered when planning my demise. At the same time as focusing on my death, I would feel extreme fear and panic that I would stay in the horror of hell through all eternity after my death. I was living in hell on earth with my mental illness and did not want that hell for eternity. I know this one of the reasons why I was afraid to take my life. I did not want to live in hell forever, and I did not want to upset God by choosing the time of my death, which is his job. I assumed I would live in torment for eternity in hell as my punishment from God for taking my life. I now feel very differently. As a strong and stable believer, my sense is that God understands when someone takes their life. I believe he is there to provide grace in that moment whether someone takes their life or changes their mind. He is there in every moment.

I have come as a light into the world, that whoever believes in Me should not abide in darkness.
John 12:46

The Holy Spirit Bails Me Out

I read somewhere many years ago that when the Holy Spirit is faced with someone considering taking their life, He brings in a truckload of guilt. A mind full of guilt that can sway one's thinking from death to life. Guilt can help one remember all the reasons to stay alive. I don't recall who or where this idea came from, but it made sense to me, so it stuck with me.

I had many plans and schemes. Once I was a foot away of hanging myself. I found a strong pipe in my parent's basement and found a strong rope. I tied the rope around the pipe, made a noose, and placed it around my neck, tightened it, and then stood there. I became emotional. I could not understand why I was standing there ready to end my life. I took a step off and dangled, swayed around, one foot still on the chair, barely.

The uncontrollable emotion and guilt flooded my thoughts. I was able to regain my balance and clumsily stepped back on the chair. I untied the rope and went off to the university for band practice. As I sat in the university band practice, I was overcome with what went wrong with my life. I was so different. Once I was a proud musician, now I was in hell.

Hanging? Electrocution? Drowning?

On another occasion of this relentless torment of depression, electrocution was the method of choice. I was going to take a bath and let the radio fall into the tub. I took a lot of baths but could never go through with pushing the radio into the water. A different plan might be easier, something that did not require courage.

I was a good swimmer in high school, I was on the swim team. I planned an incident where I would drive to an inland lake, in Pewaukee late at night, and remove my clothes and start swimming farther out than I could return. One night, I executed the plan and started to swim but came back later barely making it. Experiencing life threatening fear increases the heart rate, making it hard to catch my breath. God guided me to turn back yet again.

These are only a few examples over 15 years of suicide planning. I planned for two weeks to jump off the 21-story building where I was working as a janitor. I took the elevator up to the top floor when I was on a break. I opened the window, stepped out, and stood on the other side of the railing and looked down at all the lights. I cried uncontrollably. I stepped back inside the railing and went back to work.

Peaceful Sailing Trip

A few family members and I went on a sailboat trip across Lake Michigan. I think I was in my late 20's. While other family members slept in the cabin, I sailed the night shift, planning my death. I rehearsed it in my mind, just slipping into the water and slowly sinking deep into the foggy lake. I tied off the steering mechanism (the tiller) and stood up to position myself at the rear of the sailboat. Suddenly, my dad poked his head out of the cabin to ask me if I was okay.

After we crossed the lake in the sailboat on the Michigan side, my parents continued on their journey. My brother, his wife and I returned on a car ferry. I thought about how I could not face coming back to Milwaukee. Panic attacks ruled that day. Could I jump off the ferry and not be seen? Who knows? I did not try it; again I failed. I was so discouraged with who I was. I was incapable of living or dying.

The next attempt was a three-hour car trip to visit my grandma in Illinois. Planning my death by opening my car door and falling out, being run over by a semi. It was always panic attacks leading up to my decision. When I looked at mom while she was driving, I had guilt feelings for how she loved me.

Hopelessness in Daily Tasks

One thing that I was able to do within this state of despair was to get a job. I was able to drag myself someplace and be responsible on minimal levels. Every day, though, I thought of death. All day long, it was the only thing I thought about. Working was a helpful distraction as I tried to concentrate on my work. I could keep jobs longer when I was depressed but not when I was manic.

One day my only friend called me up and said that he wanted to go play video games at a local bar, so we did. Sounds like a simple common occurrence, but this was a big deal for me. This was the first time I could remember that I had fun while in the deathly snare of depression. I am a competitive person and that day I was competitive for no reason except that it was fun. I felt like a normal person. I frequented this bar when I was manic but never in hopelessness.

The sad thing is that friendships only occurred when I was manic and then I had lots of them. But when depressed, I spent much of my time home in my room watching television. When I watched a movie it would brighten my spirit and make me very emotional. It felt good to feel something.

Church was a blur, I could not identify who God was. Surely He was not in my life, as death ruled my thoughts – how could God let that be? Of course I wanted to believe that the reason why I was so sad was that I was supposed to be, or because I did something wrong. But still, everything turned into despair.

Why do People Ignore Depression?

I know my family saw the different mood swings, but nobody understood what was happening inside me. No one would tell me, "You will come out of it, you always do." Why are people afraid to talk about depression or give someone encouragement? Depression isn't contagious! If you suspect someone is depressed, encourage them, say a prayer with them. Remind them that God really does love them, reach out – *DO SOMETHING*.

I would have appreciated some encouragement or a hug, instead of denial. I know that it's hard for family or friends to know what to do. It turned out that I was a burden to my family. Were they tired of my behavior? They ran in the opposite direction for many years and did not help me, no compassion. When I was manic on occasion they would help and bail me out of something, but when I was depressed they did nothing. All that nothing made me feel like they didn't want me, didn't care or didn't want to know what I was going through. It was easier to ignore me, so they did. When one is depressed and realizes that even their family does not want them, it makes things worse.

The Good News !

Suicidal depression left me in 1992. I was 36 years old, and for the first time in 15 years I did not suffer suicidal depression. The six-month swing was gone and has not come back. In 1992, I finally changed psychiatrists to one who watched the therapeutic level of my lithium. For me, being on the therapeutic level took away my swings into the deep dark abyss.

I felt it one morning, I noticed things were different. I woke up and no longer suffered from suicidal depression. I woke up early and I was going out for a jog. After that, I went to buy some coffee and then I wanted to reapply to the university. I knew I was not manic, I was normal and it felt great.

Why is light given to him who is in misery,
And life to the bitter of soul,
Who long for death, But it does not come,
And search for it more than hidden treasures
Job 3:20-21

The horror becomes peace for those who get the proper help professionally with medications, therapy or both. I believe those who succeed with suicide have a place secure with God as long as they believed in Him and had Christ in their heart. To say this another way, if God wants us from this world He will take us.

An interesting and positive aspect of living in the depths of depression, I was obedient to God. I had no interest in addictions or immorality. I was able to follow a path of Godly living, in contrast to mania which always destroyed my decision-making and threw me head on into disobedience. Yes, suicidal depression removed all the addictions in my life. Why? Well, as you can expect, depression did not make me a better man. I behaved more appropriately because I was too weak to do otherwise. I had a broken spirit. I had no confidence. I was in hell in my thoughts and obedient with my actions, but what a cost of such a demoralizing existence.

God has reasons why He keeps us alive; it is not up to me to play with His game plan. When I think of all that has happened to me, I'm glad I did not take my life. I would have missed out on so much.

Therefore be patient, brethren
until the coming of the Lord.
James 5:7

Chapter 6: Many Addictions, A Constant Battle

... for the flesh lusts against the Spirit, and the Spirit against the flesh: and these are contrary to one another, so that you do not do the things that you wish.
Galatians 5:17

The Fog Clears, Mania is Cravings

God teaches us to flee sexual immorality. Catching a glimpse of a bathing woman is not sin. When we fail to take our eyes away, sin develops. Lust gives birth to sin and full-blown sin brings forth spiritual death. I have been taught this is scriptural. My bipolar illness through mania brought a starving man lusts of the flesh, which developed into addictions that would not let go for 24 years. As with any of my addictions, a little was never enough to satisfy, in fact – the craving is never satisfied, one always wants more.

Bipolar Disorder means Sex Disorder

My crude and off-the-charts sex drive was only controlled in recent years with the correct medication combination that controlled so many of my other bipolar symptoms. I have heard that some people with the illness have little to no sex drive. However, in the things I've read about bipolar, the extreme craving for sex is more the norm with us, and it's really hard to control because this is a normal part of life. One can find ways to stop alcohol, pot, cigarettes and other drugs and completely abstain, not the same with sex. Then there was the easy access to porn when I got a computer ten years ago. That's a whole other addiction to tame.

In many ways I went from a very poor defeated person to a prince in thinking and behavior when I went from depression to mania. The change happened within a few days.

Darkness suddenly into light. It would have been great if it would have stopped there, but it did not. I gained a profound way of talking and thinking. I have been told I could talk people into things and was very charming, not taking no for an answer.

To anyone I met, I seemed to be an exciting man about town, life of the party. Imagine a poor person filling the shoes of a prince. During these periods, I was a charming magnet for women. It did not matter who I became interested in, they were interested in me, or I charmed them into it.

When I was not manic, I thought I was a horribly immoral man. In the frame of mind of depression, I thought that all my misery - I had coming to me. I did not know that my illness drove this craving. The easiest way I can explain it is that sex became a meal. When we become hungry we eat. When I would get an itch I would find a woman and satisfy my craving.

My impulsive sexual cravings and affairs started in my 20's, when my illness was in full force mode, not medicated. Not being medicated means the mind can soar up in a moment and find a way to get what it wants. I'm like a ball player on steroids, I seem to be able to do things that are otherwise unnatural, and not good for me.

In some ways I became even more prideful and disobedient to God by having more than one affair at a time. Pride is idolatry, doing something that means more to us than God's will. This was only one aspect of my illness that would drag me into the devil's web, with no mental ability to get out. Habits, bad habits had consumed me in my behavior with women. The alcohol, pot, and cigarettes came and went more in binges in my 20's and 30's. I suppose I used those to try and cope with the mental illness in my brain that was relentless.

Hitch Hiking

It was the 80's, I had still not been prescribed any medications. I impulsively took my high energy and decided to hitchhike to New York. I was in my early 20's. I hit the interstate with the clothes on my back, my music case and my trombone. I had just left fellow musicians in Iowa where we had played as part of a Civil War re-enactment over a weekend. I remember playing as a quintet over a tea party, and then as the music for the evening dance. It was a fun gig.

I had an itch to travel to New York City to see my sister and her husband who lived there, so off I went. Pretty stupid thing to do, but that's mania - no planning just impulsive energy, in my brain and my body. I was soon in Ohio, truckers were nice to pick me up and give me rides. The beautiful night sky was erupting in colors as I walked, waiting for my next ride, but physically slowing down.

Suddenly, a convertible skidded off in front of me, jolted me awake out of my daze. The car was painted red with white interior and the driver looked like Marilyn Monroe. Certainly it felt like a scripted moment, just like in the movie, American Graffiti. She asked, "Where are you going?" I told her "New York City." She smiled, "Great, get in." She said I looked thirsty, so we pulled off the freeway to find a liquor store. We bought beer, vodka, and snacks and then back to the interstate.

I remember the feeling of the air flowing over the car on a warm evening; it felt so good. We drove east for an hour and pulled off the highway to a motel that she knew of. The first thing I remember when we got to the motel room was my long hot shower, so good it felt to get the dirt of my travels off of me. After that, the beer tasted great.

My driver took a shower too. When she came out of the bathroom she had only a towel in her hair. We both enjoyed talking to each other. She drank the vodka, I drank the beer, too much of both. We talked about life and other ponderings that one has when drinking. Soon we both became sleepy, so we slept. In a few hours we awoke in the middle of the night and things became heated between us. I told her we shouldn't be messing around unless we were married. Wow, a glimpse of morality while manic, how did that happen?

So I got an idea, a wacky manic idea of course. I proclaimed, "How about we use the Bible in the nightstand and recite verses and marry ourselves?" I said, "You are a blessing to me because you picked me up on the freeway. When I was very tired and hungry, you came to my aid. You are a very beautiful woman, someone I would like to have, to share my life with, after I get back from New York." So, we recited verses to each other on and on like that, and eventually pronounced that we were married. We had a wild time in bed before exchanging phone numbers and she left on her own and drove away.

She had no intention of taking me anywhere near New York. I was not the only one with cravings that night. I told her I would call her when I got to New York City. Oddly, we stayed in touch for many years. When someone told me that it is impossible to marry yourselves, I felt very stupid for what I had done and for telling anyone about it. I may have a chemical imbalance of the brain, but I can still be amazed at the stupid things my brain tells me to do that are things I would never do when I am stable. This one was definitely an unforgettable experience for many peculiar reasons.

I suppose there is a reason why mentally ill people are called "crazy". We do crazy, insane things when the mental illness controls our brain. A sad thing is that when my brain is acting like an offline computer, it also tricks me into believing that I am fine both mentally and physically. Therefore I don't seek help. I understand this is common with many who struggle with mental illness.

Flee sexual immorality. Every sin that a man does is outside the body, but he who commits sexual immorality sins against his own body.
1 Corinthians 6:18

Powerful Cravings for Alcohol, Pot, and Cigarettes
Having addictions usually means you have more than one. I had many. At times I was able to abstain for periods of time. This is confusing because it's extremely hard to quit any addiction. Sometimes I can stop something, other times no

matter how motivated I am, the addiction gets worse and overtakes me.

In recent years, God has healed most of my addictions and I am thankful. I certainly don't have the strength or discipline to quit any of them on my own. When I am closest to God and trust in the incredible strength of the Father, the Son, and the Holy Spirit inside me, unexplainable things take away my thoughts and cravings. Having the right psych meds and a great support system cannot be overlooked either.

I stopped smoking marijuana for 4 years when I drove a truck because I liked my job and did not want to fail any of the random drug tests. Shortly after I opened my business again and quit driving, the marijuana cravings came and I hid it from my wife and many others for years. My wife would say that I looked high or was acting stupid or some other accurate description of what was going on and I would get angry and deny it always. I have no idea how I hid the smell or never got caught, my wife's hearing and sense of smell is extremely sensitive.

The reason I liked to smoke pot was because it calmed me and I felt I was able to relax with it. I could work with it when I reopened my carpet cleaning company. Many days on the way to my office I would take some drags, it was my cigarette during times when I did not smoke cigarettes. Pot was my hidden drug, my secret. Did I smoke on my way to business appointments? No, I did not, my success at work was important to me. However, if I knew I was in the office all day, I did. I see now that I used it to calm the stress of running the business in addition to the low grade manic that was always with me even after I was well medicated.

I had stopped drinking alcohol in 2001 when my psychiatrist prescribed an anti-psychotic medication. I tried a shot of brandy while playing cards with friends. I didn't like the way I felt after even a little alcohol. I enjoy non-alcoholic beer from time to time and thank God for taking that craving away.

I found out years later that stress is very bad for my bipolar illness and stress is what I had when I stopped trucking and tried to build my second carpet cleaning company. Going from a pay check twice per month to being self-employed and going deep into debt instead of having income was too much stress. All of a sudden the clients I had built up weren't buying. At the end of a week, or a month, I could not give my wife a check. We ended up getting a home equity loan to fund the business for the first year and a half. The business never paid it back.

My home situation was not so good either. I was working long hours and when we would see each other it would be difficult at best. Adjusting to being married for both of us was hard. When we married, I was 40 and my wife was 36, we both had many years of being independent and not having to answer to someone else. She worked three part time jobs in the early years of the marriage, so we were broke, exhausted and angry when we were able to see each other.

I decided to lose myself in my business and my addictions. I had stress at home, yes I did. Did I have stress at work? Yes I did. My answer was to smoke pot. I hid this from everyone for about six years, until I had my pulmonary emboli episode where my doctor told me that any kind of smoking would kill me. God knows sometimes that he has to take severe action for us to obey.

One Battle Left?

With all the other vices gone, I have turned to cigarettes when under stress. I like them so much that I have a hard time quitting. I start and stop and start and stop. When I was getting divorced, I started smoking. Months later I switched to the e-cigarette which was very successful for awhile. My mother was dying last fall, so I started smoking again to calm myself. There's always a good reason to start, but tough to quit.

I can't smoke, it cuts off my circulation and causes foot pain, my neuropathy fire is horrible, but that is addiction. I already have damaged lungs from pulmonary emboli and clots in my legs from my clotting disorder!!

I turn to my faith first in this battle and hope to soon report that I am not smoking for good. I am so confident in his grace so far with my vices that I know winning this last battle is only a matter of time when I lean on Jesus. I have no desire to smoke marijuana. I expect to never again look at porn. I know that I will not ever masturbate due to my high level of pain medications and the tubular nerve damage in my groin that make it physically impossible. God's grace has taken these from me, I am so blessed.

Faith is The Way to Peace

I have a stress relaxer, my faith in Jesus Christ. This brings me such peace of mind, which can relax me instead of the addictions relaxing me. My peace also comes from having finally a psychiatrist and psychologist and other doctors who teach me and remind me to relax.

The right medications, the right therapist, they all are part of the picture. When we can relax and find peace, we function at a high level, and have more strength. At the writing of this in 2012, I have been on the only medication combination that has controlled me such that my addictions are almost gone. My craving for pot and porn, alcohol and women, all gone. God is good, though he had to go to extremes at times to get my attention. I had addictions that controlled me. Isn't that what addictions do, control us. When we have faith, medications, and a support system to take back our control, the sunshine comes out and the peace of mind becomes peaceful control.

Finally I Feel Forgiven, The Burden of Sin Is Lifted

It was January 2004, I was on my death bed with lungs full of blood clots. The pastor who came to give me last rights said, "Do you want to pray to have your sins forgiven?" I did want my sins forgiven, I became overwhelmed by the horrible wrong and immoral things I had done. I had hurt others so much, especially my wife in horrible ways. When I prayed and asked God to forgive me for my sins, it was the first time in my life that I felt I was cleansed from my past. I have always had a strong faith, but this feeling was amazing. All of the women and other addictions and sins were forgiven and I felt it deep into my soul. The feeling was one of washing, cleansing and healing a deep wound. Peace.

The way that I understand addiction is biblical. Anytime you do something outside of God's will on a regular basis, it is an addiction. What happens with an addiction is the heart becomes hardened and the addiction flourishes without asking for forgiveness. I understand this now, I enjoyed my addictions and did not want to stop. I did not stop to ask for forgiveness. This angers God.

To open their eyes,
in order to turn them from darkness to light,
and from the power of Satan to God,
that they may receive forgiveness of sins
and an inheritance among those who are sanctified by
faith in me.
Acts 26:18

I know that as a stable, Godly man, I will always ask for forgiveness when I do something wrong. I see myself on the edge of a cliff on a very high mountain. God promises to keep the wind and storms from reaching me. I feel protected and forgiven when I ask for it. I pray for a life of stability, but I make no claims about what can happen if my mental illness takes over again in the future.

God tells me every day to trust him and he will keep me from harm, and be with me if harm comes. Satan is very smart as he brings me all sorts of temptations to draw me away, but I stand strong more and more. It's not my strength, it's God's strength within me. It took me 55 years to get here and I am very capable of staying here for the rest of my life under His control and attention. I am capable of this with my vast support system of doctors, medications, and people in my life who care. But that does not mean that I am not tempted and that Satan does not stop coming to test me.

God also comforts me when other people judge me for my behavior. This passage from John 8 encourages me that Jesus forgives me.

They said to Jesus, "Teacher, this woman was caught in adultery, in the very act." So when they continued asking Him, He raised Himself up and said to them, "He who is without sin among you, let him throw a stone at her first."

When Jesus had raised Himself up and saw no one but the woman, He said to her, "Woman, where are those accusers of yours? Has no one condemned you?"
She said, "No one, Lord." And Jesus said to her,
"Neither do I condemn you; go and sin no more."
John 8:4,7,10-11

A Bipolar Christian?

Every year would come and go in my life. I would always have an inner desire to grow deeper and deeper in God's ways. Stating that I am a Christian is a big deal. Saying I am mentally ill and a Christian is another thing. People who know that bipolar and other mental illness can mean addictions and immoral behavior at times is a problem. Those who don't understand mental illness think that I am making such horrible behavior choices. Christian people who should not be judging can at times be the strongest judges of things they don't understand.

So, what is the real answer to being a Christian who is mentally ill? - Which sometime means one who sins more than the average church-goer. God states that when you accept Christ into your life, you "know my Son Jesus Christ then, you will get to know me and I will give you the Holy Spirit." That means mental illness or not. The Bible does not say that if you are mentally ill, you are not forgiven, you are damned to hell.

It does not say that you are exempt from knowing Jesus. Opening myself to the Holy Spirit within me was a key turning point, I was no longer fighting, I was surrendering and allowing healing and forgiveness.

So I say to you, ask, and it will be given to you;
Seek, and you will find;
Knock, and it will be opened to you.
Luke 11:9

If I had my way I would ask Jesus just take me up into heaven and away from all of these addictions, and mostly away from the pain throughout my body. I had a new pain medication added a few years ago that put my mood into a hypomania, lower level manic that turned on the addiction lightbulb. This time it was sexual thoughts overcoming my mind and cravings for porn in addition to other side effects. Karrie noticed weird behavior, such as not walking back into the bedroom at night after using the bathroom because I was sleepwalking. I am so sensitive to medications, I became manic enough to be a problem after only a few of the pills.

Sexual thoughts poured into my mind (I thought I was rid of them). Did I like them? Sure I did. It was an addiction that I had most of my adult life, but after two weeks, I had enough. I wanted them to go away and I knew I was powerless. I reached for my Bible and asked Jesus to help me in my distress. I opened the Bible to Galatians 5:24. *And those who are Christ's have crucified the flesh with it's passions and desires.* The verse told me to put all passions and thoughts on the cross and I did that with my whole heart and mind. This time I was desperate to rid myself of this curse, so I really meant it when I begged the Lord to take it from me.

Instantly, the flood of sexual thoughts went away. The sexual rapid fire impulse brought on by mania can come on like a runaway train that seems fun to ride but is just crude and strange when looked at through normal eyes. I have no explanation for why I have not had sexual thoughts since this day. That's what faith is, - belief when there is no evidence or understanding.

We need to look at sin like one of those bug zappers we have on our porch. There is a light and a bar and the insects are attracted to it and when they touch the bar they die. Just like sin. When we come to Jesus with a problem, we know it gets zapped and we are forgiven and it is no more. Having an intimate relationship with Jesus allows us to grow closer with Him and when we grow closer to Him, He grows closer to us.

We grow in confidence and trust. He is always here for us even in sin with addictions. We end up in sin having an affair then ask Jesus for forgiveness. Satan has convinced us that pleasures to the body are okay and we deserve to have them. A mentally ill man or woman needs Jesus to put out the addiction. Well, we all need Jesus, but that's not the focus at the moment. When we call out to God for His help with an addiction, He hears us. It is up to Him how He will bring the addiction to a halt.

Faith saved me more than once with my addictions, I wanted to be obedient and did the best I could. That is all Jesus expects, to want to serve Him. Jesus will teach us how to withstand the temptation.

But if we walk in the light as He is in the light,
we have fellowship with one another,
and the blood of Jesus Christ His Son
cleanses us from all sin.
1 John 1:7

Being Stable Solves So Many Problems
It is 2012 as I write this, and I am taking great medication for my mental and physical illnesses. I still need help from God though, and I know he brought me my new psychiatrist and psychologist. All this help does not mean that I am free from the cravings of my addictions that come calling. I do my best each day and I am at peace.

Chapter 7: Near Death or Near God?
My Body is Sick Too

Lord, make me to know my end,
and what is the measure of my days,
that I may know how frail that I am.
Psalm 39:4

Concave Chest Surgery

I was a junior in college, I was 21 years old. Dad approached me and reported that he had found a surgeon who could perform surgery to repair my concave chest. I was studying to become a professional trombonist and I had a problem. My lungs could not expand properly, I was unable to play higher notes. I agreed, and I was hoping that I would die on the operating table because I was in a suicidal depression.

There were complications on the operating table, but the operation was a success. For recovery, they put my bed with the heart patients. There was no room left on the unit where they intended me to go.

I was told that I coded in the middle of the night, which prompted the nurse to come running. The nurse was not aware that I wasn't a heart patient. She quickly put a pillow on my chest and told me to wrap my arms around it and pull down, which she helped me do. She assumed I was a heart patient, that is what they do with heart patients. The damage was done quickly, my chest was crushed back to how it had been. The skilled surgeons work was a disaster. I ended up with a surgical scar the length of my chest, with numbness and discomfort and a concave chest for the rest of my life.

In the days that followed after my discharge, I was at home. I was not healing correctly, the more I walked, the more pain I felt. It became so bad that I could not breathe. Dad drove me to the hospital and every bump felt like an explosion in my body. He told me to be brave. I just cried in agony on the inside. When we arrived, the doctor knew exactly what to do. I had pleurisy, water in the lungs.

The surgeon numbed my chest and then tried to insert a long tube in my rib cage. He lifted me, my whole chest was up off the bed. Then suddenly, down I went on the bed. He had failed to insert the needle into my lungs. He tried again. This time he put it between my ribs and I cried out from the pain. I asked for pain relief, so he gave me a shot in my thigh. Within seconds the pain was gone. At the same moment, the fluid came rushing out filling two large containers. Finally the torture was done, and I could relax.

I began to feel better. It was spring where the season turns to mania. The suicidal depression was gone, I felt the warmth of life. Because of the surgery, I was very weak in my chest and it was difficult to put on pants and tie my shoes. I went to the UWM pool and walked widths of the pool, again and again. This allowed me to rehab myself to regain my strength and flexibility. Manic energy was actually a help.

Pain Tolerance Isn't Easy

God knows my tolerance of pain, which is very low. I have learned to trust God with what He allows to come my way. Medications don't always take away my severe pain. I am resistant to taking more and more and more medications as my body gets accustomed to whatever I am taking, which always then requires taking more. That's a slippery slope of a lifetime of a lot of medication. And of course, the more I take the more likely it will make me manic which I don't want.

I am a wimp with pain, I hate it, but I try to cope. In addition to prayer, and focusing on the Bible, I have learned biofeedback principles and have my own version of what my psychologist taught me. Once I got the hang of it, I use it and it really helps me. Hurting every day with chronic pain, tends to be more difficult on the mind than on the body.

I go into a room alone and sit down. I look across the room at an object. I visualize that the object is the image of

Jesus. I ask Jesus to bring me peace of mind. Then I take my hand and physically push away any negative thought, emotion, concern. Be it a relationship, a circumstance, something with work, I keep pushing it away from my mind.

I do the same thing with physical pain, I take my hand, push the pain out my mind. I keep focusing on Jesus instead of the pain. I do this until I have total peace in my mind and body. Then, I sit there and let it wash over me and take hold of me. I have found that when I am able to keep peace of mind, it is much easier to make decisions in my daily life. I have deep peace from the biofeedback whenever I take the time to do it.

I Can't Breathe !

In January of 2004 I was 48 years old. I was outside on the driveway trying to push the snow blower in a bad storm. I became weak and had trouble breathing. I assumed it was the wind and the cold in my lungs. Soon I could not stand and crawled on the pavement to our back door. I barely made it inside.

It was a Sunday, we spent the day going to three different urgent care locations. One was about to close due to the weather, another had so many people in the waiting room, and the third one turned us away after concluding that I had asthma and needed to go get an over the counter inhaler and I would be fine. The inhaler was a joke.

Monday morning I was having more trouble with talking and walking around. I called to get in with my primary doctor, they could not fit me in until Tuesday. My wife felt that I was not able to stand or walk to the car and asked if they had a wheelchair at the office for us to use when I got there. That appointment never happened. I tried to get to the bathroom on Tuesday morning. After taking over an hour to crawl there, I fell to the floor trying to use the toilet. My wife called paramedics, they had oxygen that I needed to even talk to them. They took me to the hospital by ambulance.

I was in the emergency room for three hours; they were having trouble diagnosing me. I was receiving oxygen, and with it I could breathe normally. They wanted to send me home and my wife told them to have me walk around without the oxygen. She had made her mind up that we were not leaving there to go home. I was not able to walk around without the help of the oxygen tank. At that point, my primary care physician came in and took control of the situation. He told them to order a CT scan of my lungs right away.

Soon I was in the intensive care unit because I was having massive pulmonary emboli (blood clots) filling my lungs. I was not expected to live through the night. I had to have an emergency procedure to install a Greenfield Filter in the main artery in my abdomen to keep the clots from going up to my heart, lungs and brain. My pastor came to give me last rights. I waited in my hospital room to see if I would live. The surgery was a success, but that's still a big scare and the problem was not solved, my body was still making clots. I would live on a blood thinner and see hematologists for the rest of my life.

We had planned to go on a vacation in early February. We had saved money and planned for a couple of years for it. Nothing fancy, a resort in Florida to relax. We had to get our money back, and I have been too afraid to fly on an airplane since then, due to the risk of clotting. My health and it's affect on our marriage and finances has permitted us only to take car trips to my parent's summer place in Door County.

The next morning after the surgery, my wife found out from one of the nurses that I was on Ativan to help me relax and sleep. She explained that I have an opposite reaction to many drugs and requested that they not give me any anti-anxiety medication because it might make me manic. She had seen me get manic on an allergy medicine that was supposed to be sedating, and the same reaction to Nyquil. This would start a long pattern of medical people not listening to her about how my mental illness is affected by medications.

The next day I was up walking the hospital with great energy, eating like a horse! Karrie again tried to change their minds, but was unsuccessful. I spent two weeks in the hospital, regained my strength and with the manic energy was ready to go home. The anti-anxiety medication ended at discharge, so I was off it cold turkey, not good for my mental health.

Recovery Takes a Strange Twist

The effect of the sudden med change was immediate. When I arrived home after the blood clot scare, I did not want to leave the house. I never had this side effect from going on or off a medication. I now understand that this is called agoraphobia. All I knew was fear, phobia, and panic attacks on a paralyzing level. I was afraid to drive. When I did have to go somewhere, I could not go in. I only went to bank and pharmacy drive- thru service and nowhere else. I was in a deep depression of phobia. It took five months before I could start working at the office again, so I worked from home. My office was a place I liked to go to and it was only a mile from our house and I could not make myself go there.

My phobia was so bad I could not walk into a building by myself for two years, nor drive on the freeway alone. Having someone with me, I could do both. This fear was so real, I could only walk away as a coward. I logically knew the fear was irrational but it did not matter, I had no strength to fight it.

After almost two years of hell and misery, I found a manual on the internet about phobias and extreme anxiety. I started to read it and practice the exercises recommended. Slowly I was getting better and feeling hopeful.

Around this same time, a friend of mine sent me information The 4 Spiritual Secrets by Pastor Dick Woodward. The 4 secrets have a similar theme and are very simple. At this writing you can find them at www.4spiritualsecrets.com. When I read "I can't, but he can. I am in him, and he is in me," I was instantly able to internalize it. Christ is in me, and I am in him. This makes anything possible, it made me think of Philippians 4:13.

I can do all things through Christ who strengthens me. Philippians 4:13

I got it immediately, I understood and the timing was both perfect and critical. I was desperately ready to be done with my fears. I visually and mentally felt the healing presence of God as I repeated it, *I can't, but he can. I can't but he can. Since he is in me and I am in him, I can!* It's such a simple, yet powerful concept that I use it often when I am frustrated or going through anything that seems hopeless or when I need to overcome something I don't have the strength to deal with.

I decided to put my new confidence to the test. I went to Walgreen's to pick up my medications. This time I would try to walk in and not use the drive-thru. I had not gone in for almost two years due to my ridiculous fears. I was in the parking lot and recited to myself, "I can't but God can as He is in me and I am in Him." I entered the double doors and the next double doors and kept walking with no anxiety. Now I was screaming "yippee!" on the inside.

Next I drove to the freeway the entrance ramp, I recited again "I can't but God can as I am in Him and He is in me." I drove 45 minutes that day on the freeway. I was set free, I did not want to stop driving.

Depression, suicidal depression, anxiety, phobias, panic attacks and, fear, are too consuming. They are the dark side of life. We become inward, helpless and defeated. I have experienced all these. What is the answer? Go outward. Ask God for His help and timing so that through others you can be led to doctors, medications, faith, maybe a church.

For me, finally getting Geodon has been a great part of the answer for me. It motivates me without being manic because I am not drugged and tired. I now take Geodon and Lithium, but that may need to be changed in the future. My psychiatrist explained that most of his patients are well balanced with Geodon. For me, I feel more like myself than I ever have with Geodon. I can just be John, I can have my personality without feeling like a drugged up mental patient. My ex-wife says that I have more motivation, I am able to do things that require thinking or learning that I had not been able to do before.

Brain Aneurysm Surgery

I collapsed in a parking lot in October 2004 and was rushed to the hospital. They found bleeding in my brain, and it continued for two weeks. I was told that they could not find anything else wrong with me. So, they were going to send me home once the bleeding stopped. One doctor thought that somehow my bipolar illness was an issue; he determined that I was faking when I would not walk and cooperate with physical therapy due to my extreme level of pain and inability to walk. He had rehab come in to get me ready to go home. One day they came in and put a gait belt around my waist and insisted that I walk 10 feet. My balance was so off. My legs didn't work, they were like jello, no strength. My legs had been twitching and wiggling around since I collapsed, at times they moved around like I was riding a bike in the bed. The area of my brain affecting my legs was where the aneurysm was eventually found.

During the initial testing, there was too much blood to see what was going on in my brain. They kept me until the bleeding stopped and did the tests again. After about two weeks in the hospital, they did the tests again and found an aneurysm was tucked behind my right eye.

Surgery was scheduled to clip the aneurysm. They had to shave the right side of my head, open up my skull and go to work. Many hours later they successfully clipped the ballooned blood vessel. They put everything back in place and stapled my head together. I am so lucky to have a nice head of hair, the scar is a bit nasty. I remember when I was recovering for two months in the hospital, I was combing my hair one day and it got stuck in a staple they missed.

Prior to the surgery, I asked my parents to call my younger sister in Tucson, Arizona. I thought I might not make it through the surgery and I wanted to see her. She came and stayed with me around the clock after surgery. It was such a blessing to have her there, everyone else had been sleep deprived for a couple of weeks. My older sister made her presence felt by coming to the hospital almost every day, once I was able she did leg exercises with me in my bed, she is a dancer by training and knew how to help me. I am close to my two sisters. They are very special to me. Living with a bipolar brother has not been easy, they don't know what to do or think at times.

Pain medications in large quantities cause mania. In my case, during this hospitalization, the meds caused delusional dreams, hallucinations. The best way I can describe it is that you close your eyes, and then when you open your eyes, you truly believe that what you are experiencing is real. I experienced these dreams for six weeks because I was being over medicated before and after the surgery.

My wife tried her best to explain to staff that I have bipolar disorder and that they were over medicating me. The medical staff would not listen until four weeks into my first hospital stay. My wife met with the hospital administrator. She pleaded for the team to either contact my psychiatrist or to have one of their psychiatrists involved because I was very manic by this time which was becoming unsafe for me. I had been removing my IV, the feeding tube, and the heart monitor wires.

Jesus Comes to My Aid

Hand restraints kept me in place on the bed at times. I could not press the call button for the nurse. Talk about feeling helpless. I woke up terrified one night, panic attacks crippling me, fear over taking me. I was strapped in my bed and unable to speak because of the breathing tube. Something caught my eye to the left and Jesus was there. As soon as we looked into each other's eyes my fear went away. Total peace washed over me. Months later I was reading in the book of Joshua where it speaks about being strong and courageous, not terrified because Jesus is with us.

Have I not commanded you?
Be strong and of good courage; do not be afraid,
nor be dismayed,
for the Lord your God is with you wherever you go.
Joshua 1:9

Finally the staff psychiatrist contacted my psychiatrist. Meds were adjusted, the traumatic dreams stopped, I stopped ripping out my tubes and wires. I stopped jumping around on the bed trying to leave. The restraints that kept me tied to the bed like an animal were removed.

Should John Live or Die?

Of the many tubes, I had a breathing tube in my throat due to my breathing difficulties. My lungs were damaged from the pulmonary episode nine months earlier, so I had pneumonia on and off too. Normally they like to take a breathing tube out in a few days, but I could not breathe on my own after 2 weeks.

I had a new reason to be terrified because the medical staff told my family that my breathing tube had been in for too long. My family needed to make a decision the next day. The medical staff reported that because the breathing tube had been in for so long, that family needed to decide to either get a trachea in my neck or remove my breathing source and allow me to die. My family wanted to go home and pray, give their answer in the morning. My family met, without including my wife (who is my power of attorney) and they decided that due to my lifetime of suffering, to pull the breathing tube out and end my life, which they ordered my wife to do.

My wife did not agree and felt that God was telling her to keep me alive, so she sought out the surgeon who did my brain surgery. He said that I had complications, but putting in the trachea would be a safe way to resolve the issue. So that is what they did! They cut a slit in my lower throat and the healing began. It took serious effort on my part to learn how to breathe again with the respiratory therapy, but I did it.

On to Recovery or Divorce?

I went in and out of mania in my two-month stay in two hospitals. As soon as I was stable, my wife had me moved to a hospital where my primary doctor could see me and that was a teaching hospital that also was next to a psych hospital. So, it was assumed that they would also be more experienced with mental illness. I did get better care at the second hospital. I was a complicated case and I think the first hospital needed a break from me.

This was a difficult time with my wife. I asked for a divorce in the hospital, which triggered to her that I was manic. I ask for a divorce whenever I am in a higher level of mania. I had everyone convinced in my manic ranting that it was real, so my friends and family were shunning her. She did not need that on top of everything else that was going on. She was working as much as possible so that she would not lose her job due to all the time off she took, which was becoming an issue.

On little to no sleep most nights, she was daily tending to my needs in the hospital as well as rehabbing a vacant house that we were trying to fix up and sell. We were flipping it to have money to pay for my long hospital stay in January when I had my pulmonary surgery. She was also running my small company, dealing with uncooperative employees. They were so frustrated with the situation that they vandalized my office.

My wife became suicidal herself for a short time, had panic attacks when driving and was losing the ability to keep all the obligations going. She sought out medications, it did not help. She wrote a letter to friends and family asking for help and they just called her crazy and lazy for doing it and ignored her instead of helping.

The last week I was in the hospital, I had plenty of energy though I could not walk. The rehab team was very nice at this hospital. They taught me how to walk properly, I had a lot of speech therapy, and other daily living skills. I was primarily in a wheelchair. I was only able to walk very short distances, with help.

Only a week or two into my rehab, a meeting was held to discuss my status and plan for recovery. I was told that this would be the first of many weekly meetings or progress updates. My parents and my wife were there in addition to eleven other health care people. Numerous doctors, nurses, rehab staff, social worker. Each person gave their report on how I was doing. At the end, the social worker stated that I would be discharged and sent home the next day. 24-hour supervision was required for at least a few weeks, maybe longer.

My wife just about lost it, this was the straw that broke the camel's back. She was already at the end of her rope. She certainly could not miss any more work to stay at home with me, and I was in a wheelchair. No home services were available 24/7. My parents stepped in. They offered for me to live with them for the remainder of my rehab. Everyone was still under the impression that I wanted a divorce. We were now in mid-December, holiday season in full swing so people were distracted with other things.

Dad took me by wheelchair out to the car when I was discharged. The first place we went to from the hospital was my office. It was good to be somewhere familiar. We stayed for two hours. Then we went to my parent's condo. My parents allowed me to stay for eight weeks. I will never forget their kindness.

My dad was a great rehab drill sergeant. I was in a wheelchair for only a few days. I went to the walker, then the gait belt, then walking on my own. The long hallways with handrails in the condo building were perfect for my rehab. I remember the hardest thing to learn to do was to take a shower, getting in and out. Very scary feeling when your balance is gone. By the time I was physically ready to go home, I was no longer manic and wanted to go back to my own home and my life.

The residual effects of the brain aneurysm are that I get pain and headaches on that side of my head if I don't get a lot of sleep. The more serious effect is that I have peripheral neuropathy throughout my entire body, worst in my legs. Lots of pain medication is required to endure it as it worsens.

Hernia Surgery

It was in July of 2006, we were in the process of bankruptcy. I had just celebrated my 50th birthday which was a big deal because it was not certain if I would live to be 50 after the pulmonary and brain episodes.

I was closing my nine-year-old carpet cleaning company in the process of the bankruptcy. I was a bit down about our circumstances that never seemed to get better. I had been having strange severe pain in my groin and went in for an ultrasound, I had a hernia. Not a big deal for most people, but with my neuropathy, the pain for me was horrible and there was a wait for the surgery. The doctor put me on very strong narcotics for pain and told me I could not drive for a couple of months until the surgery.

I was in misery, but it was summer so I sat on the deck and prayed a lot. The surgery came and went, but something was wrong. The pain persisted and my groin turned blue after about two weeks. I went back in for another ultrasound and they found the problem. An area had filled up with fluid and the pain was humbling. I asked the surgeon how long for the tissue to drain, he did not know. It took four months for the tissue to drain.

I was not working, could not drive, but elevated manic because of the pills. Just a simple little hernia surgery. I know that God uses suffering to teach us obedience or get our attention in some manner. It is my sense that he allowed me to have the hernias and the tubular nerve damage in my groin to discipline me and put my body and my mind right so that I would no longer crave porn, masturbation, and women in an addictive manner. God's efforts were successful.

... yet He learned obedience
by the things which He suffered.
Hebrews 5:8

Blood Clots in My Legs

During my manic episode in 2010, I ended up in Toronto, you read about that trip in Chapter 2. During that two months, I had stopped taking all of my prescriptions, including my blood thinner that controlled my clotting disorder.

After two months, the pain in my legs made me want to take my life. It wasn't until I slowed to a halt and prayed, that things changed. My ex-wife answered her cell phone and immediately came to my aid to get me medical attention.

Inspired by the Spirit of God,
If we allow the Spirit to work unhindered in our lives,
we can draw upon His guidance and wisdom
in all areas of life.
1 Chronicles 28:19

I had been praying for compassionate doctors who understood the bipolar illness. When my ex-wife and I arrived at the walk-in clinic, I could not walk, barely could drop into the wheelchair. The doctor who greeted us was very compassionate. I told her of my inner thigh pain and basic medical history. Tears welled in my eyes, I was in so much pain and weak. She ordered an ultra sound to be done immediately to check for blood clots. Finally, after numerous hospitals and clinics thinking I was just crazy or drug-seeking, someone who wanted to help me.

The tech doing the ultrasound mistakenly thought that I was about to die when she saw all the blood clots. The doctor did not feel that hospitalization was necessary, so she ordered that I get back on my blood thinner and added Lovenox blood thinner injections for the next five days.

I slept for a couple of weeks. Although my hematologist explained a few weeks later that the clots in my legs were a mix of old and new, it is still life-threatening for me to stop taking my blood thinner, clots could have gone elsewhere and killed me. He said that I am very normal for someone with a clotting disorder, but I needed to stay on my medications. God continues to deliver me from the trouble that my mental illness gets me into when it tells me to stop my medications.

... God ... sent His Angel
and delivered His servants
who trusted in Him....
Daniel 3:28

Chapter 8: Health Professionals - Father Forgive Them, They Know Not What They Do

God often waits until the last moment
to rescue His people. Will we trust Him even then?
Esther 8:12

Psychiatry, or a Guessing Game?

In 1992, I was 36 years old. I changed psychiatrists and was prescribed double the amount of lithium, a step in the right direction. I had been taking a low dose that was not enough for seven years. It was better than nothing, but I was hypomanic and full of addictions and bad decision making.

Over the next nine years, with more medication, I did not experience a bipolar swing of suicidal depression or mania, so I was indeed better. But certain addictions controlled me. I was having affairs with women. Sexual thoughts, pornography and marijuana distracted my thinking. My psychiatrist seemed to enjoy my reports of sexual conquests and hearing how much I was smoking pot to cope. He never seemed concerned about the behaviors I talked about, so I wasn't concerned either.

I even had an affair with one of his resident psychiatry students who lived in the apartment above me. He always asked for the details, it was very strange. I only needed him for medication refills a few times a year, and I am not one to question people of authority. Now I look back on it and I am angry and disappointed at the care I was given (or not given as the case may be).

After nine years of being under his expensive care that my insurance didn't cover, I became manic and had my very first psychiatric hospital stay for eleven days in 2001. I got in an argument with him (that is what most manic people do, pick fights and have arguments) and I fired him. I would think there would be some "do no harm" code of ethics, such that a mentally ill patient cannot fire his psychiatrist during a psychotic breakdown. I have a tendency to hate, or piss off, or get rid of all the good people in my life when I am manic. Shouldn't that be a sign that I am manic? Shouldn't an experienced teaching psychiatrist know this?

No, my psychiatrist, whose office was just a floor below me in the psych hospital that I was at, refused to see me during a real crisis. Isn't there some kind of oath or internal compass that someone should have if they go into psychiatry? I give him my hard earned money for nine years and he did not educate me about my illness or really help me in any way. He wrote prescriptions but was not there for me when I was a broken mess. I just don't get it.

Firing doctors happened many times when I was manic. It wasn't just the psychiatrists, but medical doctors too. Then trying to get them back when I come back down seemed impossible.

My first psychiatrist lasted 15 years, 7 years with no meds, 8 years with not enough lithium. The second psychiatrist lasted nine years prescribing lithium only, but finally at a therapeutic level.

My third psychiatrist was found by my wife after I had the first hospital stay in 2001. I needed a new psychiatrist of record for follow up. For nine years, that psychiatrist took better care of me. She listened to my wife's reports of my behaviors and educated both of us about my illness. She explained things to do and not to do with medications and lifestyle. She was available on those rare occasions when we needed to call between appointments with a question. She prescribed lithium, Zyprexa, and later, Depakote. She tried others, but settled on those. I had severe side effects to many that we tried.

She was as motivated as I was to find a way to reduce or eliminate the hand tremors I have from the lithium. I forget the combination she found, but I was without hand tremors for only a few weeks when a manic episode landed me in the hospital again in 2008 and I had to be put on a stronger cocktail of meds again to be stabilized. I have had the hand tremors increase ever since.

I took Zyprexa for nine years. It is an anti-psychotic that was for me also used as a sleep aid. It worked for nine years. I later discovered from other psychiatrists that Zyprexa is best used more for short term crisis management and not long term use for someone like me.

I fired psychiatrist number three during the erratic, irrational, and of course impulsive manic episode of spring 2010. She was already planning retirement, so I had needed to find someone new. She had a good no-nonsense manner but was thorough and helpful.

My fourth and fifth psychiatrists came next in 2010 and 2011. The fourth was recommended by the psychologist I started seeing in summer 2010. Another step in the right direction, psychiatrist #4 taught me more about myself and my illness and so genuinely wanted to help me. He changed my medications to only lithium and Geodon. He got it right and I am so thankful. Geodon is keeping me the most level I have been in my life, with the ability to be motivated, but not manic. It gives me a clear head to think and be at peace with myself. I felt too drugged for many years. I thought I was lazy or it was the mental illness that made me lethargic. I think it was the medications. I am more myself than ever before. Another miracle from God. I am so thankful. With a clear head I can do so many things, like write this book or have confidence. I also have more strength I need to put up with my physical pain.

Thank you Jesus! Thank you for new medications and doctors who are not afraid to try them! I am like a new and different person. His career took another direction and he referred his clients to others. He connected me to my current psychiatrist who is also a rare and caring man who is taking good care of me. He is another one who treats me like a valued human being. He is open to working with my ex-wife to watch my moods and wants me to be the best John that I can be. He is not just there to refill prescriptions and treat me like just another crazy patient.

As I look back on the years with psychiatrists, I wish I had changed at times when I knew things were not right. I was weak, I did not have the courage to stand up for myself. It's likely that I would not have suffered so many years with no meds or the wrong meds. I also held all doctors in high esteem as experts that knew what they were doing. Now, I trust my own instincts and know that God wants better for me. I speak up and make changes when appropriate, when I am stable, when I know what is best for me and what is not.

Do I Really Need a Psychologist?

It wasn't until 2008 that it was recommended at discharge that I needed an on-going psychologist. I was being discharged from my second psychiatric hospital visit. I had gone thirty years with psychiatrists and rare visits with counselors/psychologists, most of which did not seem worth the time spent. The first one wrote in a note pad the entire visit while I talked, no interaction at all. I don't need to pay to listen to myself talk. The second psychotherapist, she was similar but I was hypomanic during the period of time I saw her, so when she would make a suggestion, I was not really interested because I was just being manic and disagreeable.

I had a good relationship with the psychologist I started with in 2008, she worked in the same office as my psychiatrist so they could compare notes and work together, which was extremely helpful in 2009 and 2010 during manic episodes where their help was needed when I refused to show up for appointments. She educated me on things about my illness, ways to cope with stress. She was more available via phone and e-mail on those rare occasions when my wife or I had a concern or question. Of course after all their help, I fired her and the psychiatrist during the manic episode of 2010.

My current psychotherapist is a man I respect, and he respects me. He is an encourager. When I ask him for feedback, he shares things that help me. He has gentle and sincere manner. He really wants to know me and challenge me to be a better person. The session is give and take, he is a wise experienced psychologist who provides profound feedback that I need to hear.

For me, the most important part of our relationship is God's presence in it. My therapist is a man of faith, a man of integrity. He is not quick to judgment. When I discuss my struggles, he always tells me I deserve better and helps me stand up for myself. He has helped me think positively and improve my self-image. He is patient and willing to explain things in a new way when I don't understand. This relationship I now consider to be an important part of my on-going management of my life and my mental illness. Find a good counselor if you need one and keep looking until you find the right one!

Caregivers Who Don't Care

Unfortunately, I have a lot of medical conditions that have landed me in many hospitals and clinics. As soon as they are aware of my bipolar diagnosis or psych meds, they treat me like a nutcase or a criminal. Assumptions are instantly made that aren't fair or warranted. If my brain is offline from time to time, would that not warrant more compassion instead of less?

During my 2010 manic episode, I was taken by police to our local psych crisis intake. I was indeed manic and needed to be tied down to something and forced to take my meds. While in the waiting room, I had heart palpitations that resulted from a few sips of one of those energy drinks earlier in the day. My fragile body can't handle these drinks, or alcohol or caffeine for that matter. So, the psych intake staff sent me to a nearby hospital fearing that I was having a heart attack.

The nurses treated me horribly for no reason, again. They knew I was on 72-hour psych hold from the county psych unit, so that meant I was a piece of meat that could be mistreated. As a godly man, I must forgive them, but it gets old when this treatment happens on a regular basis.

A nurse came in to put in an intravenous needle. I have had this done many times. I looked at what she was doing on my arm. She had inserted the needle, but had not capped it off. A pool of blood the size of a baseball was on my sheet and she was smiling at me in sort of a devilish smile and I knew that dark forces were involved. It was the devil that was trying to piss me off, and he was again working through the nurses. I said, "When are you going to cap it?" Only after that did she do it. There was a lot of blood on my arm and the sheets. She taped over it with clear cellophane tape that didn't stick because she did not wipe my arm off, and she left the room.

The next nurse said I needed a second IV. I explained my request to not have it placed at a certain spot on my wrist because of the extreme pain and that they can't get a good line there. I have little skin there and they can't get a good line there, I know this. She denied my request and put the needle there. Again, the area was taped over using clear tape covering the blood. No clean up, not even an alcohol wipe. Within a few minutes, my whole arm was red, swollen and filled with pain. Of course no one answered when I pressed the nurse call button.

A third nurse came in because she recognized my parents who were there by this time. She went to our church. She removed the needle from my wrist, cleaned up my blood-stained arm and reinserted the needle properly. She cleaned up both arms and apologized. God was sending the people to fight my battle when I could not. They did tests, abused me some more and discharged me back to the psych intake.

Cuckoo's Nest or Psych Care?

My ex-wife and I waited eight hours at the psych intake for them to admit me. She stayed because she was there with me in 2008 and knew that the intake waiting room was a bit of an abusive cuckoo's nest experience. With my medical problems, it was not safe to be sitting in a room with many other unstable souls and ignored for many hours. The strange things that went on were much worse than the movie and I was glad she was there. After all those hours of waiting, they said I could sleep in a bed overnight there. I would be transferred to a different psychiatric hospital in the morning. Even after we were divorced, I kept up my additional insurance. Though expensive, it allows me to go to good quality psych hospitals when necessary.

So, at 1:00 am, I was going to a bed and my ex-wife went to leave. The nasty security guards had told her hours before where to move her car, far away if she was staying awhile. They stated that she would be escorted to her car when she left. Well, it was pouring rain, very dark and horror-movie like outside and they told her she would be fine and showed her the door. They were not processing any new people or anything, they were just too busy watching TV from their post to care about her safety. She had to run up a hill and around near the freeway and back into a now vacant dark parking area, knowing that the property she was on was populated by mostly unstable crazy souls. She was sane and normal, and she was treated like crap also. I guess working in a crazy house makes the workers misbehave as well?

Medical Doctors Don't Know Psych

My body chemistry is very sensitive to new medication. I become challenged by side affects. Unfortunately, medical people seem to understand medicine interactions that affect normal people. But there seems to be little to no knowledge of how many medications, especially pain medications affect those with a mental illness. Many times I can have a psychotic reaction whether I am on psych meds or not, my chemistry is just different. When I try to explain this to medical people, they think I don't know what I am talking about and they know better. I am the one that pays the price by becoming manic or suicidally depressed. Then they try to blame it on something else.

In 2006 after my first hernia operation, my neurologist took over for pain management and at one time I was taking seven different kinds of medications for pain twice per day. Anxiety meds, muscle relaxants, sedatives. I was not only a zombie. I became irrational and argumentative with everyone around me. When I complained about all of the medications he had prescribed and how I was feeling, he removed five of them cold turkey without weaning me. He had no suggestions of anything to replace them. That left me as a vegetable in severe pain and depression.

The Vitamin D Fiasco:
Are the Milwaukee Brewers for Sale?

I went back to that neurologist for my yearly check up, it was 2008. He prescribed vitamin D for energy but the quantity he prescribed was 50,000 units a week. A psychiatrist later told me that most bipolar patients can't handle that much. That well-meaning doctor put me in a psychiatric hospital for a week as I became highly manic, very fast.

When I took 50,000 units for my second dose, I went off the rails within hours. I entered a high mania. All of a sudden increased energy, I woke up in the middle of the night and drove off. It was 2008, we were still married. I did not come home for two nights. I was driving fast to nowhere as usual when I am manic. I stopped by a friend's house for a card game and I had brought alcohol. I was already off my meds, very high and liking it. Mania is fun in the beginning. Not having any self awareness that you're driving everyone else nuts is also great.

The next day I needed to buy a fishing license to go fishing with a neighbor. I had not been fishing in years, but psychotic impulsivity makes no sense. When I arrived at the store to buy the license, I noticed the used fishing boats on his lot. After I got my license, I bought an old fishing boat for $1100, with $500 down. The agreement was that I would pay it off and take possession in 30 days. That detail will be a key legal detail later. So I started showing up and working on fixing the boat. I was familiar with boats after working with my dad on them, so this was not totally foreign to me.

On the same day I bought the boat, I thought it would be fun to have a sports car. I went shopping. I ended up at a BMW dealership and noticed a convertible. I was wearing a Milwaukee Brewer baseball hat. I convinced the salesman that I was planning to buy the Milwaukee Brewers for just under a billion dollars.

Then we test-drove the car, I was up to 120 miles per hour. It is likely that I was also driving erratically and dangerously at that speed. The salesman should have been able to see that all of this behavior was not stable. When we returned to the dealership, without a job, no credit check, I put down $500. I promised to pay off the $22,000 in 30 days and then take possession. When I returned home, my wife went through my wallet to try and determine where I had disappeared to. She saw the receipts for the boat and car. She ran to the bank just before they closed on a Saturday morning. She tried to repair the damage that had been done to our account. The money I spent was for bills that had not yet cleared.

She was able to get the car dealership to refund the down payment $500 back to our account a few days later, they were understanding of the circumstances. The boat dealer was not understanding and wanted his money. My wife contacted attorneys, a local TV consumer advocate and filed complaints with state and local agencies and he would not back down. Since we never took possession of the boat, eventually the complaint to the debit card company was voted in our favor and we got part of the down payment money back months later.

Within days, I ended up in a psych ward on my birthday. I was supposed to have a party and then go to a Brewer's baseball game, but instead I was in a psych hospital thanks to Vitamin D.

Everything is about Bipolar

My journey in life too often revolves around my bipolar mental illness. Trying to understand the depths and heights of the illness is impossible while not on medication. The brain has a chemical imbalance that cause an inability to make correct decisions. Reality becomes a lost subject. We look at a doctor as one who knows how to help us, yet sometimes I have experienced, we do not get the care we seek. Misdiagnosed illness causes the inability to treat with the right medications. Even with the right diagnosis, there are many meds and everyone reacts differently to each.

Not testing for therapeutic levels is another problem that some doctors do not oversee properly. Therapeutic testing monitors that we are taking the correct amount of medication. By taking medication everyday and being monitored by a spouse and getting monthly check-ups by my doctors limit problems that can occur and creates a happier fulfilled life for me.

The work of righteousness will be peace,
And the effect of righteousness,
quietness and assurance forever.
Isaiah 32:17

Forgiveness is the Answer

As much as it is hard to do, I have to forgive. I must forgive the health professionals, the church leaders, the family members, the friends, and myself too. When they hurt me to the core of who I am, yes it is painful, a pain of rejection and judgment that I don't deserve. My mental illness has driven me to do some very bad things that I would never intentionally do when stable, but I have done them. God has forgiven me for some horrible sins, so who am I to deny forgiveness to others.

I also know that many who have shunned me or judged me, they do so out of ignorance, impatience, or maybe lack of compassion. Regardless of the reason, we all do our best at times in our relationships and we get it wrong. Unfortunately, we live in a society that is quick to judge, and we are all harsh on each other.   In addition, the average person does not understand mental illness, and one's lack of control over it at times.

I want others to forgive me when I need to be, so I work hard to forgive others.   Forgiveness also gives me peace. I talk to Jesus about it and let him and his Father deal with these people and judgment of their behavior toward me.   That is a big emotional relief.

For if you forgive men their trespasses,
your heavenly Father will also forgive you.
But if you do not forgive men their trespasses,
Neither will your Father forgive your trespasses.
Matthew 6:14-15

Chapter 9: Bipolar Disorder - Helpful Things I Have Learned

A wise man will hear and increase learning,
And a man of understanding will attain wise counsel.
Proverbs 1:5

What Is Bipolar Disorder?

Many people are unaware that there are different variations of the illness. I will share with you simple generalities that I have learned. The clinical details for any professional are much more complicated to consider in diagnosis of a patient, so always seek professional advice. First of all, bipolar of any type is part of a group of diagnoses called mood disorders.

Bipolar I is often characterized by more manic episodes and behaviors than depression over time.

Bipolar II is the presence of more depression than mania over time, will not actually have a severe manic episode, but does include low level mania, called hypomania.

Cyclothymia is chronic and numerous high and low moods. Shifts in mood are more frequent but less severe. This includes fluctuating low level mania with low level depression. This is a pattern over time, of at least 2 years.

Bipolar NOS (not otherwise specified) is a term I will leave to the professionals. It basically means a mood disorder that has bipolar characteristics but does not meet all of the clinical criteria for one of the above.

More detailed diagnostic information on these and all other mental illnesses can be found in the American Psychiatric Association's bible, the *Diagnostic and statistical manual for mental disorders, (4th ed., Text Revision) or the DSM-IV-TR (APA, 2000)* if you are so inclined to read the clinical jargon.

More Terms to Know

Hypomania – lower level mania, a milder form of mania, same symptoms but less likely to include psychosis or impaired functioning.

Mixed Episode – both the symptoms of major depression and mania happen during the same day, every day for at least a week.

Rapid Cycling – four or more mood episodes during a 12 month period.

Mania – a severe episode lasting a week or more that can include reduced need for sleep or food, grandiose ideas, self-destructive and extreme pleasure-seeking, fast talking, racing thinking, inability to control impulses, easily distracted, inability to sit still, lack of self awareness, poor judgment, inaccurate perception of reality, psychotic religiosity, hallucinations, irritability.

Major Depression – severe low mood that can include loss of enjoyment or interest in most things, loss of ability to work, significant weight loss/gain, insomnia/hypersomnia, loss of energy, hopelessness, inability to think or concentrate, thoughts of death/suicide. I remember reading somewhere that the rates of suicide are greater with bipolar depression than with those who suffer from major depression alone.

Symptoms Are Just Words

In my stories you see how bipolar disorder has affected my thinking and behavior. The mind is very sick indeed when not stabilized with medication. I've already talked about how the irrational thinking combined with a complete lack of impulse control leads to addictions.

From my perspective, some of the terms used for bipolar symptoms are just words. To one who has to experience it, it is hell. For example, racing thoughts does not begin to describe the racing freight trains in my mind that collide and switch tracks all at the same time, all with different topics and thoughts that are unrelated. Then the pressured speech tries to unload these out of the mind by dumping all the thoughts, one after another. The problem is, the faster you speak them and dump them, the faster more will come. The feeling that you will burst if you don't quickly unload every thought and idea is quite overwhelming. A manic person can keep these incoherent rants up a long time.

Where does Bipolar Come From?

The experts tell us that there is most often a hereditary nature to most mental illness, bipolar included. In my case, someone in four different generations of my family line have had either a type of bipolar, or other mental illness.

If the hereditary genetics for the illness are present, then bipolar can be triggered by a stressful life event. It is also possible for someone to carry the tendency for bipolar and not manifest it if such life stressors do not occur.

Treatment and Support

I have mentioned my feelings of the importance of medications as well as a support system in the goal of being as stable as possible. This can look different for every individual. I encourage that you seek out help and don't try to struggle with it alone if you are experiencing any mental illness. Find others who have been through it and gain from their knowledge and experience.

Continue to seek out the right doctors and counselors until you get the right ones for you. Some people find that support groups work better for them than individual therapy. There are organizations that provide more of a community support. They will have resources, assistance in applying for disability and other services that may help. Still other organizations provide social activities or help in getting employment.

Your local *National Alliance on Mental Illness* (NAMI) office is a good place to start, because they offer so many different programs. Mostly free services are offered for those with mental illness as well as separate programs for family members of someone with mental illness. NAMI has a local group in many large cities. Their website is www.nami.org, and we recommend checking the website pages devoted to NAMI FaithNet. NAMI's national toll free information helpline is 800-950-NAMI. A great deal of information and resources can be found online. Calling or visiting the office nearest to you will encourage you about the extensive services available in your community.

Another large organization that will lead you to resources and information is the Depression Bipolar Support Alliance, find them online at www.dbsalliance.org. Their toll free number is 800-826-3632.

Many other excellent and helpful magazines, books, websites and groups exist. The two organizations above and their websites will lead you to so much more. A good amount of information with both of these groups is offered in Spanish. Once you reach out and see what is available, you will feel encouraged by others who experience what you do, and learn from them.

Some of Our Favorite Books, Magazines, Websites:

- **bp magazine**, www.bphope.com, 877-575-4673

- **I Am Not Sick, I Don't Need Help!**, by Xavier Amador

- **Codependent No More**, by Melody Beattie

- **Loving Someone With Bipolar Disorder**, by Fast &
    Preston

- **We Heard the Angels of Madness**, A Family Guide to
    Coping with Manic Depression, by Berger & Berger

- **Married to Mania**, downloadable book,
    www.marriedtomania.com, by Elizabeth Atlas

- **100 Questions & AnswersAbout Bipolar Disorder**
    by Albrecht & Herrick

- **What Goes Up: Surviving the Manic Episode of
    A Loved One**, by Judy Eron

- **Touched With Fire: Manic-Depressive Illness and the
    Artistic Temperament**, by Kay Redfield Jamison

- **Night Falls Fast: Understanding Suicide**, by Kay
    Redfield Jamison

Video/DVD
    (available from Netflix and other sources)

Mr. Jones, TriStar Pictures, with Richard Gere,
    story by Eric Roth

Boy Interrupted, HBO Documentary Films,
    by Dana and Hart Perry

Shadow Voices: Finding Hope in Mental Illness,
    produced by Mennonite Media for the National
    Council of Churches, www.shadowvoices.com or
    www.visionvideo.com

The Church & Mental Illness

As much as I rely on my faith for coping, I know that there are some Christian and non-Christian churches that don't think people should see a therapist or psychiatrist, or should not take medications. I have run into such well-meaning but uneducated pastoral counselors, pastors and other church leaders. These well-meaning people haven't a clue about how serious mental illness can be and how difficult to manage in the best of situations.

My feeling is that you would not tell someone with cancer to just get their act together, or to pray for healing and not seek medical attention. Yes, prayer is important. However, recommending that church-goers not seek medication or therapy that they need, is very wrong, in my humble opinion. I have been shunned and asked to leave by pastors when I thought that a church was one place where I would be accepted. I never did anything strange or violent, they were just afraid of what MIGHT happen when they knew I had bipolar disorder.

Your connection to your faith can be an important part of coping with any illness, but don't be discouraged if you don't find the understanding and support for mental illness in every church. Just as with medical professionals or others in your life, keep going until you find what you need. Be at peace that it's their difficulty or ignorance with mental illness, not your fault.

Mental Illness is not a Choice

Bipolar disorder, and other unstable mental illness states of mind are psychotic and horribly irrational. Impulsive, uncontrollable decisions and unintentional poor judgment combines with a lack of any common sense. When I am unstable, my brain does not compute consequences, it does not weigh any behaviors. My brain is like a computer that has crashed because you took an ax to it. Something may come up on the screen, but it isn't going to work.

No matter how many times someone tells me to get my act together, my brain does not understand what that means. Come on – why would one choose to drive a car without gas, think they can buy houses, boats, and cars truly thinking they can afford it with no money in the bank? No one would intentionally choose to skip eating, sleeping, drinking for days.

You Can Do This!

Mental illness, when treated with proper medication and a support system, allows one to have a very normal life. I personally benefit from God being part of my support system and I highly recommend it. Society too often equates violence or whacky behavior or homelessness with mental illness. There are plenty of doctors, lawyers, musicians and other occupations filled with those whom you aren't aware of who have mental illness and are well managed and quite stable with medications much of the time.

Preventive care is essential with mental illness, but even the best laid plans can go awry when something unexpected or unknown causes the brain to misbehave. Be honest with yourself, your caregivers, and those close to you. Share how you are feeling with someone. Others can help to watch out for you when you cannot watch out for yourself.

Being embarrassed or ashamed will not get you the help that you need. I know now that I personally need to watch for mania in the spring/summer season like many others with bipolar. I did not learn this until 2010, talking with my new psychotherapist. I also must be careful with pain medication changes. In addition, I require a lot of sleep. Everyone is different. If you or someone you know is struggling, reach out.

When wisdom enters your heart,
And knowledge is pleasant to your soul,
Discretion will preserve you;
Understanding will keep you.
To deliver you from the way of evil
Proverbs 2:10-11

Chapter 10: Blessings & Hardships

Rejoice in the Lord always.
Again I will say, Rejoice!
Philippians 4:4

The Good, The Bad, and the Ugly
> Through the ups and downs of mental and physical health challenges, I have come out bruised and battered but my spirit remains strong, well – most of the time. Good thing that God is patient and kind. He created me with the bipolar illness, so he needs to put up with the ups and downs that my illness creates.

Each day something happens that makes me grateful though, gives me cause to rejoice in the Lord. It is not about what I want in worldly success, possessions or good health. I trust him now to meet my needs whether things are good or bad or ugly. He does meet my needs, as promised in the Bible. I have been in the peaks of playing my music with superior musicians and in the depths of despair, tied down to a hospital bed ravaged with fear. Regardless of the situation, once time has passed I see God's hand in the events.

The Good
> Counting my blessings helps me focus on what I do have instead of my losses and lack as compared to other people I know. It's quite easy at times when I am sick or weak or a little depressed to focus on the lousy aspects of my life. My list of blessings reminds me how well I have endured and that I do have much to be thankful for. Try it some time, the change in focus can be uplifting.

God's Plan For My Life
> For so many, many years I stubbornly kept opening carpet cleaning companies because I was afraid to do anything

else. I could not make it as a musician, no longer had good enough health to drive a truck, I knew nothing else – so I thought.

In 2010, God took my business from me one last time. In a big drama with unsavory characters, my company van with all of the equipment in it was stolen, all appearances point to an employee. I did not have the strength or health or finances to start over yet again. I finally gave in to God's plan to get me away from the stress and drudgery of these ventures that were rarely profitable. This time I had spent much of my divorce settlement money trying to keep the company running, which did not work. It was the grandest of blessings that the company was done, gone. I wish I had heeded the signs sooner, God tried many times to get me out of my business and on to something else, I was always so afraid.

I know that You can do everything.
That no purpose of Yours can be withheld from You.
Job 42:2

As an adult man, my identity was very wrapped up in being a business owner, doing something that I was truly good at and respected by my clients. Now that the business was gone and I made peace with that, I was restless for a time. The next step was to change my entire lifestyle around, being honest about my limitations, and not worrying about money. That was not so simple, it was a process. I did my share of moaning and complaining.

I now take great care of my health, I allow myself to sleep a lot which I require, and I no longer apologize for it. My focus is my e-mail ministry, the message of this book, and my new work at a local hospital. I work as a volunteer chaplain on the unit where brain injury patients request prayer or visit from a chaplain. I am doing God's work in all roles. For any of these activities, I can participate when I am able to.

My Social Security disability income is enough to pay for most things I need. My ex-wife takes care of the household needs. We have little, but we still tithe to churches we support. We live paycheck to paycheck, there is often not enough to truly take care of our needs. We are so blessed, there are people in our lives who provide for us when we have a need and we are so extremely grateful. God continues to provide for us in unexpected ways.

My life is low stress and enjoyable. It took so long for God to get my attention and move me to where I am now. I am at peace. I never would have chosen any of this or even dreamed it up, but God did.

My Faith is my Foundation

I have talked at length about my faith as a cornerstone of what allows me to be at peace and cope with my hardships. I have also mentioned many examples where I could later see God's protective hand around me when I was manic or depressed. There have been times where I saw God immediately in a situation and am amazed at the risky or dangerous circumstances where he protected me against the odds. His presence to keep me calm in dangerous situations has kept me alive. I accepted Christ into my life when I was 19 years old, this is likely the biggest blessing of all.

On one of the occasions when I was in New York City trying to be a musician, I went into a fast food place in Times Square. There was a long line. Two men near the front were harassing a woman. I put down my trombone and walked up to see if she needed help. The two guys, thugs by any definition, continued to explain how they intended to harm me when I left. They were big and scary indeed. My brain reasoned that I was likely dreaming, and if not, God would take care of it.

I had no one to call, no cell phones then. I was alone and no one would know if I went missing, no one to call if I was injured. It was difficult to eat my food with them yelling threats in my face as I ate. I was very hungry and hoped they would leave first. It was unusual, how calm I stayed. Normally when manic I would have been picking a fight just as strongly, and likely suffered the consequences. God kept me quiet.

The manager had called the police. The police came in behind these thugs and stood there listening to them threaten me. Eventually they walked over and casually put both in handcuffs. The manager said it was the first time she could remember the police actually being able to get there to resolve a call. She said to me, "You must have an angel with you." I calmly replied, "Thank you, yes I do. His name is Jesus."

For I am not ashamed of the gospel of Christ,
For it is the power of God
to salvation for everyone who believes,
for the Jew first, also for the Greek.
For in it the righteousness of God is revealed
from faith to faith;
as it is written, "the just shall live by faith."
Romans 1:16-17

Encouragement Ministry E-mails

I suspect that I get more enriched in my faith by sending my regular Bible verse e-mails, than do the people I send to. The process of being in the Bible daily and meditating on what to say to others truly saved me in 2006 when I was in despair, unable to work. I was wallowing in self pity in my pain, waiting for my hernia surgery. Sending the e-mails kept me distracted and focused on God.

I have appreciated the replies I receive, and how others say they are touched by the simple few sentences of a message. I feel such joy when someone writes, "you were really speaking to me today, that's exactly what I needed to hear." Sometimes I ask for prayer for someone, but always include a short Bible verse that people can digest in the few moments they have. I know many people read it at work and are busy. I hope my e-mails remind them to keep God close to them in their day. It's hard to believe I have kept it up all these years.

God Shows Me a New Calling

Almost two years ago now, my ex-wife was in graduate school, getting her master's degree to be able to work in the mental health field. Anyway, in one of her classes she was sitting next to a chaplain from a local hospital. She found out that they have a volunteer pastoral care program that included a class, certification, and then the ability to work with patients.

We were both interested, but she was too busy to add more classes or volunteering to her stress load. It took a few months, I finally contacted the hospital and filled out what seemed like an endless amount of paperwork for the application process. I went for the interview that was two hours. I was initially told to wait outside the door at the end of the interview. Soon I was told I could join the class but on probation. They were concerned about how much I talked, I was just nervous.

I went to every class, even though my mother was dying, and died during the time frame of the class. I wanted no one to have an excuse to hold me back from getting the certificate and working with the patients.

A few weeks after mom died, I was visiting patients and in one room was a woman who looked very much like my mom. She was the same age, height, hair length and her smile. We talked and she told me she was going to die, but she was going home to live. She was a Sister of Notre Dame, an esteemed group that lived nearby.

It was the ease she put me at while we talked. I asked her if she would like me to pray and she said that would be nice. I left feeling happy. Hours later when I was done visiting, I had grown tired and was sitting in the lobby of the hospital. There she came, in her wheel chair, all full of smiles and waving her hand just like mom would. I gained so much from that visit.

But that wasn't the end of it, after the class and practice experience, I had to calmly wait months after finishing the class to start working with the patients. I am normally a little impatient about such things. I knew God's timing was perfect and I needed to finish this book and God would make it happen when he wanted me to be there visiting patients. I now go weekly to the hospital and talk to the patients in the brain injury unit where I can relate to many of the patients and what they are feeling.

Sailing

I have not said enough about the years I enjoyed sailing and it's positive effect on my life. I have not been able to sail a sailboat since 2004 when my medical conditions left me very weak. Since the brain surgery, I have been too weak physically or mentally to handle a boat or the quick reaction and decision-making necessary for sailing.

Sailing was relaxing for me, being out on the water. It built confidence for me, I was good at something that not everyone could do. It was also a social outlet. Getting friends together to go sailing was something I did often. One of those social events on the boat allowed me to meet my wife.

I remember one night when I had ten friends on board, a perfect warm summer evening. We took a tack out heading south for about an hour. I taught others how to help me sail the boat. We hit wind and it was fun to heal over, so the port side and the cockpit of the boat are next to the water and starboard is way up in the air. We were moving four or five knots.

When I decided to head back, I noticed the mast light flickering. I went into the cabin to check the power source. I turned the switch on and off, on and off, no lights came on. We were sitting ducks if other boats couldn't see us. I tried the engine, the battery was dead. I brought down the jib (front sail) so everyone could see around the boat.

God blessed us with a shift in the wind. The clouds blew away. We had a clear sky, bright stars and moon. The friends I had on the boat all were calm. I explained that we could sail back inside the breakwater, down the channel and go into the slip by pulling down the main sail in time to slow us down.

We had an air horn that one of the passengers was assigned to sound in all directions. Within a few minutes, a Coast Guard boat was coming our way. They were looking for another boat and saw us. They brought both boats in to the marina. The battery was later fixed, it never happened again. God was watching and we were safe. When I trust God and the abilities he has gifted me with, I am calm and confident.

So Many Blessings

It needs to be said, I am blessed to be alive after the many times that a physical illness or risky decisions and behaviors during a manic episode could have, should have, sent me up to heaven. God seems to want me here for reasons he knows, so here I am. There are bad days when I plead for him to take me to heaven and out of my pain, but my pleading is not what counts. When I think of the earthly things I would have missed by not being here, I am again focused on the incredible people and things I continue to experience and be surprised by.

I have talked in other areas of the book in detail about the blessings I have had with my music, my work, my marriage, and these are many. My addictions being removed from my life one by one with little or no effort on my part is a biggie. No way that I could have fathomed that, God's handy-work indeed.

Finally I have a team of caregivers around me that I trust and appreciate. Those who watch over me are my ex-wife and my family. I also am thankful for great doctors of many types, including my psychiatrist and psychotherapist who I actually look forward to seeing. The amount of hardship endured to get to this point is something not worth focusing on, though I never forget.

I am very excited about my recent round of Marcaine injections in my feet which has helped my neuropathy. My wife was reading the Sunday paper, something she has not had time to do much in recent months. She was also reading a section that she normally would toss aside. God's orchestration of events I say. This day she saw an ad for the clinic that does the Marcaine injections. I called and my insurances covered it completely. I am able to, so far, avoid adding more pain medications due to the reduction in my level of neuropathy pain. This is a big deal for me, I was fearing losing my toes or feet at some point because my condition has been worsening. The color in my feet is better, circulation is better. Wow, this is in the miracle cure category if you ask me. I can also go back for more injections if I feel the need to.

Certainly all the areas of my life that are now healed, were all horribly, painfully ruining my life at times. If I had been told that it would turn out well, I doubt that I would have believed it. God's timing is always best and I know he had to teach me some lessons, get my attention, and at times discipline me to bring me to where I am now.

So, what does God do once He has our attention? He starts to mold us into His likeness. With me, He did His best work and biggest changes in my life through hardships in the hospital.   Some were medical hospitals, some psychiatric hospitals, but each time he was there.

Have I not commanded you?
Be strong and courageous. Do not be terrified;
Do not be discouraged, For the Lord your God
Will be with you wherever you go.
Joshua 1:9

Hardships

Ok, there have been many hardships on the flip side of most of those blessings I just talked about. The stories in this book tell many of those tales. Divorce, job loss, financial ruin, surgeries, family problems. As I said, I don't want to dwell on the hardships so much. However, there are a few things that I have not discussed much, that remain a big part of my life.

Since 2004 I've had daily chronic pain from neuropathy in the bottom of my feet, my legs, hands, groin and skull. The neuropathy was the result of my brain aneurysm. The pain from the neuropathy is the reason I sleep so much, it wears me out. When my pain medications wear off, I am in extreme pain. Waking up first thing in the morning makes me want to cry out sometimes.

Hand Tremmors

This whole writing thing is a joy for me, but not an easy task. My hands tremmor, badly at times, from the lithium side effects that I have endured for 28 years. This has left me with no choice but to type with just my index fingers. Some days I have so many repeated keys, I can't type and have to stop.

People have asked me if I have Parkinson's because it's not only my hands that tremor but also my legs. I used to be embarrassed, now I just say it's a medication reaction.

Eating a meal with utensils is all together different and a challenge. I ask that my beverage is poured half full and with a straw. I don't always remember this in a restaurant and I spill. Coffee is out of the question as my hand tremor will spill it all over the place. With small vegetables like peas and corn I have to use a spoon and sometimes I just leave those alone, they fly all over no matter how hard I try. Eating a potato is okay but it always depends on the day which forkful is going into my mouth and which one misses. Because of all this I put my head down close to my plate sometimes and that looks goofy too.

When I am at home I usually use two hands to drink out of a glass. It has been an affliction that is most noticeable, and I do tire of how I have to work around it.

Hardships Are Truly Blessings In Disguise

When we are in the middle of battle, we do not always see the victories that are won. But when we look back on to them, we see how God protected us and allowed us to claim victory over ourselves. God made me so He knew what He was in store for when I was born.

As I sit today I can look God in the face and tell Him I fall short. I sin against Him but I will also tell Him that when

He puts me into His service I am willing and unafraid to complete His task. Most of my struggles are one on one with people. When I ask God for a certain relationship to be healed, He takes His time but the relationships eventually are healed and this gives me hope to continue on with His effort of bringing people to His Son. If the relationship is not healed, it was not meant to be.

I called on Your name, O Lord, from the lowest pit.
You have heard my voice; Do not hide Your ear
from my signing, from my cry for help.
You drew near on the day I called on You, and said,
"Do not fear."
Lamentations 3:55-56

Chapter 11: My Two Loves –
Marriage, and Mom

O my dove, in the clefts of the rock,
In the secret places of the cliff,
Let me see your face, Let me hear your voice;
For your voice is sweet, And your face is lovely.
Song of Solomon 2:14

Marriage

All a man could want. I met a special woman in 1995. She still loves me today as I love her. My ex-wife, who I now live with, has become my caretaker for my physical and mental health needs. She is also my payee for my finances. More importantly, she is my best friend, and I believe the mate that God has chosen for me. Not even divorce can keep us apart it seems when God has other plans. We were reunited under strange circumstances after a horrible manic episode in 2010 caused me to lose my apartment, my money, and my health.

Over the years there were numerous times when I filed for divorce, paid retainers to attorneys during manic episodes, only to cancel the divorce when the mania lifted. No longer able to take my manic behavior, addictions and manic spending, my wife called my bluff and filed for divorce in 2008, just before my brother died suddenly.

We were divorced in 2009. We were only apart for a year when I needed a place to live, and to recover from a manic episode that left me in severe physical pain from blood clots in my legs that set my neuropathy on fire.

I would prefer to get remarried, but staying divorced protects her in ways that she deserves. She is protected from future manic episodes such that she does not share the burden of responsibility for my manic spending of money we don't have. She had to work hard to get the boat and car contracts voided from my 2008 manic episode. Those dealers could have insisted that we make the payments and keep the items. She also would not be financially or legally liable for my risky behaviors that could harm someone or myself, or land me in jail or worse. If I hurt someone unintentionally, no one can sue her jointly for any liability legally or financially. For example, I can't try to sell our house while manic. I am no longer legally joint owner as spouse.

Here's Your Bipolar Husband, Good Luck

My ex-wife learned about bipolar swings the hard way, first hand. It was never easy but knowing nothing about the illness or what it could do was unfair. The circumstances made her navigate the shark infested waters of mental illness without a clue. The first few episodes of mania were sheer horror, but she did not leave me. She took the marriage seriously and tried to help me and figure it out. She hung in there when family and friends couldn't take it.

She began to learn and understand the warning signals and she was always at my side when the dust settled. One night not too long ago, before we went to sleep, I asked her, "Why do you think God put us together?" She said, "So you could bring Jesus to me, and so I can take care of you when you can't care of yourself."

I want to add that I think a reason why God put us back together after the divorce was for our relationship to heal. Healing so deep, that we could experience the kind of love, trust and friendship that marriage is designed for. This means, a love that is not confused by or tainted by or damaged by mental illness.

I am being healed of my many addictions and Karrie is enjoying a more stable mood from me. I can love her deeply, and she has less stress without the dramas. Being both stable with medications and free of addictions means I am present in the day to day of a relationship. This is new for me, and very comforting to experience. It makes me feel like a grown up adult, again a new experience for me. My mental illness, in an uncontrolled state, kept me needy and immature and unable to connect with others in a meaningful way.

I am strong it seems when she is weak, I keep her calm in the storms she endures with school, work and her own struggles. We certainly have endured hell on earth together, that seems to bond us more than any joy or good fortune. It's a sad way to develop love, but it's what happened.

I felt that when God permitted me to lose my mate, it was the lowest time of my life. I could not believe that we would or could be divorced. She did so much in our marriage. She took care of the finances too, which were a challenge at times because my income was unpredictable.   She supported me emotionally when I needed it. She was there in the psych hospitals by my side, at times living mental illness with me and through me. I suppose that's why she went back to school to get a master's degree. Her frustration with mental health services turned into a mission to try to make a difference. She is currently a mental health social worker and is looking forward to becoming a licensed therapist in 2013.

I was ill and nearly broke when we divorced. How could she allow this to happen I asked her? She told me she loved me but that I was destroying our finances and her sanity with my manic episodes. Running my business with little or no profit, always needing help from her paycheck to make payroll got old after years of that.   She simply could not take it anymore. I asked God how could this happen. He hates divorce. We were divorced.

What I want is marriage. That is what I was taught. When two people are in love with each other, you get married and stay married. My bride is there to take care of me, but it's no longer fair for her to be held liable for any more financial bailouts, surgeries, or mental breakdowns on a legal basis either.

I know God orchestrated the events that led up to our union back together, so I will honor God in my relationship with her. We both love each other much more than before. As we make our way through the jungle of physical and mental health, we trust that we will be okay because we are on God's path for us, and we don't forget it.

Karrie was learning even more about bipolar in text books and classes as she earned her master's degree in counseling. She began to understand me better as I learned to welcome her into my life and my mind. She does take good care of me and she is very good at what she does. She takes care of me when I am very physically sick, giving me shots and other cares when needed. She also is an advocate with doctors and hospital staff when I don't know what is going on. I put my trust in God that I will remain as stable as possible. With my doctor's care and Karrie's watchful eye on my behavior, the future looks good.

Stable mental and physical health means that I can be in many relationships like a normal person. My mood is more controlled, so others can put up with me and want to be around me. Being stable means I can be John, I can just be me. My personality is not run by my mental illness. I am not defined by any of my illnesses.

At times when I am going through a real tough time, I ask Karrie, "why did you let me live that day in the hospital after my brain surgery? Why didn't you let me just die?" On those days when I am in extreme pain, I just want to leave my body and go up to heaven with Jesus. She always replies the same thing, "God has a plan for you, and you're not done here yet." She had to have the courage to say no to my family's wishes that day at the hospital. She kept me alive, not knowing what condition I would end up in.

Not long after that, everyone I knew and the hospital staff were buying into my rantings about a divorce. Only Karrie knew it was just another manic symptom. So, they all shunned her, treated her badly at a time when she was trying so hard to hold it together. On one occasion when she came to visit me, my dad was looking at the yellow pages for a divorce attorney, making calls from my hospital room. She stopped coming around because there was always someone in my hospital room, either ignoring her, giving her dirty looks. I cannot fathom the pain that she endured through that difficult time. We did not get divorced at that time, I came down from the mania about a month later.

My beloved spoke, and said to me;
Rise up, my love, my fair one, and come away.
Song of Solomon 2:10

Karrie is a strong woman. However, she has her breaking point. All the stresses over the years have taken their toll. She once said, "The hardest part for me is to watch and not to be able to do much, just watch." She watched me be manic and not be able to reason with me. She watched me be mentally unstable and unable to get me the help I needed because no one believed her. She watched me be in physical pain, and not be able to make me feel better. She watched me lie about my addictions. She watched others treat me like I was a nutcase, an idiot, or a hopeless cause.

She watched me manically file for divorce numerous times, having to put up with lawyers and family members who thought it was real and pushed her to hire her own attorneys. She watched all of our money go down the drain. She watched me struggle to be normal. She watched me say my peace in the divorce court. I told the judge how much she had cared for me, and no longer deserved the burden.

There is another aspect in all of this. Karrie's life was put on hold. She had goals of being a public speaker and had just started getting paid to speak when my mental and physical health went down the tubes. She had a publisher she was working with on a book based on some of her speeches. She made up excuses to them about why she was not working on it, and then eventually dropped the project. Working full time and dealing with me was draining. The early years of all this were particularly hard when she felt very alone and confused. Extra projects were something she had no energy for.

We have learned in our relationship that she is the rudder and I am wind that fills the sails. Actually, it is God who operates through me and God who works through her. When I get upset, she calms me. I do the same for her when she gets angry, which is how she gets when she's tired, she has no patience.

We pray together, we help each other. We are very much a team now, and this book project has proved that on another level. I wait patiently for her to return from her day so that I can see her again. I love her presence, I love her spirit. I enjoy conversation with her, and being in the same room with her.

Faith is the key to our relationship and our faith in Jesus Christ. I love my sweetheart, with all my heart, mind, spirit, and soul!

Miss You Mom

I have another rudder in my life, my mother. She died in late 2011 before this book was completed. I miss her. I have dozens of e-mails from her that I've saved. In my e-mail ministry she would send replies to support and encourage me with her feedback. I like to reread them, it makes me feel close to her. We were close at times and distant at times. My mental illness seemed to have worn her out, frustrated her.

I lived with my parents on and off until the age of 35. During those manic/depressive years in my 20's and 30's I would move out. When I would lose everything and become suicidal, I would end up back home. It was a pattern that happened too many times. My parents did their best to support me. Being bipolar I'm sure was no prize for them, I could never be normal and develop or mature. I could not finish school, could not keep a job, the illness would always attack and derail me.

In those years, it was mom who bought my clothes, kept me looking good. Mom prepared breakfast, lunch and dinner, never asking for the money I did not have. She was a great cook, so I ate delicious healthy food. When we grew up on the farm, mom took good care of us kids, she was devoted to all things motherly. When we grew older and moved into the city, off mom went with dad to church. She played the organ or piano at the church. When mom played the piano, her fingers would glide over the keys and the music was emotional and beautiful.

Mom and I had music to enjoy together. She played the piano and sang while I played the trombone. We were in college together at UW Milwaukee. She worked on her master's degree in music therapy while I was in the music education program. She advocated for the music department to keep me enrolled when they wanted to drop me as a student.

We would spend hours practicing together. For some reason I often picked out classical music that was beyond my capability. Mom would have her piano part ready while I struggled with super high and fast notes. I kicked myself for years for doing that, struggling so much. What is the point of being good at something when you choose what is always out of your reach technically, and you fail miserably? I have since made peace with the areas of jazz that I excelled in and that is enough. Mom had a lot of patience trying to each me the classical aspects of my musical training that I needed.

Mom was always there to encourage me. Many times the music just flowed between us and I like remembering those successes as being very special moments when we connected.

For this my son was dead and is alive again;
he was lost and is found.
And they began to be merry.
Luke 15:24

Mom spent her life in the church playing piano, singing, composing, being a worship director and ordained pastor. Mom learned how to offer her faith, knowledge and wisdom to others. She was always a good listener too. She counseled church members individually and in group programs that she facilitated with my dad. She had many gifts that she shared with others through the church and her community outreach.

I played my trombone in the church orchestra that mom directed for 15 years. Mom picked out the music for each church service, making sure it supported the sermon message.

Sometimes when I would hear mom play or sing, it reminded me of when I was very young. Her gifts of her music and her voice will continue on in my memory and in my heart. It is a blessing for me to remember and enjoy.

My Mom has been lifted into heaven while I have been writing this book. Mom was battling three years of bone cancer and remained strong up to the end. She was in hospice care in their condo. She was so still, lying in hospital bed, on a morphine drip for comfort measures. When she turned for the worse, preparing for her trip up to heaven, we all were there. I walked up to mom, sat next to her bedside and told her, "I apologize for all the hurt I caused you, and for not being by your side as I should." She replied softly, "John, it wasn't your fault." Years of turmoil and life-long regret erased in seconds. So much went unspoken over the years.

Family members walked in and mom sang hymns with them. Mom quoted scripture verses too. Then she started going through the transformation phrase of going up to heaven and back. One time she said, "It is glorious, it is so glorious I can't even look into it." She was speaking about heaven. We are forever touched by her sharing part of her heavenly glimpses with us.

Dolores Wenzler

I share below verses from the Virtuous Wife as written in Proverbs, it describes my mother. Those that knew her well will recognize her in these phrases:

The Virtuous Wife
Who can find a virtuous wife? The heart of her husband safely trusts her; so he will have no lack of gain. She does him good and not evil all the days of her life. Strength and honor are her clothing; She shall rejoice in time to come. She opens her mouth with wisdom, and on her tongue is the law of kindness. She watches over the ways of her household, and does not eat the bread of idleness. Her children rise up and call her blessed; Her husband also, and he praises her; Many daughters have done well, but you excel them all. Charm is deceitful and beauty is passing, but a woman who fears the Lord, she shall be praised. Give her the fruit of her hands, and let her own works praise her in the gates.
Proverbs 31:10-31

I see now, my mom and ex-wife were alike in many ways. Sadly, they did not have a relationship where they could have shared their common interests and abilities. I admire both of them as being extremely strong in their own special ways. Both have cared for me when I was not able to care for myself. I am blessed.

Chapter 12: Married to Madness -
Notes From my Sweetheart

God is our refuge and strength,
A very present help in trouble.
Therefore we will not fear,
Even though the earth be removed,
And though the mountains be carried in to the sea.
Psalm 46:1-3

The message of this book would not be complete without a discussion of how our marriage weathered the various insanities of John's mental health challenges. There was so much that were misunderstood for so long. Add to that the toll that his numerous medical conditions took on each of us individually. and as a couple. Having one or the other is horrible, but the psychiatric issues affected the medical and vice versa on many occasions, and always will.

After a decade of hell from 2000 to 2010, we are now in a calm period. I pray that God has lifted us once and for all out of the deep end of the pit. However, with mental illness, one never knows. It is smart to appreciate and enjoy the good periods when they exist.

I will share some of my perspectives as spouse, although it has been hard to whittle it all down to only a chapter. There is so much to say about being spouse or caregiver to a loved one who struggles with mental illness – enough to fill a book or more.

Faith Is Our Answer – Because it Works
Our relationship suffered for most of our marriage, and ultimately was reborn after our divorce plus a host of other disasters. Only God's grace can be the explanation. We were at each other so much during those early years. I thought the

stress itself would surely put me in an early grave. My emotional and physical health suffered too. At a young age we both feel elderly, tired, just plain worn out. Our priorities have become simple now - keep God in everything. We take care of ourselves in ways that most people our age don't have to think about for another 20 years. We do what we can, but due to our constant levels of exhaustion, it's a challenge.

I still find it strange to explain to people why we now live together, still divorced, no plans to marry again in the future. I will get to that story later. But, such is mental illness. Life is not normal in all the big ways or little ways that one would hope for in life. Only our trust in God's plan for our relationship is important now. We live day to day and don't make a lot of future plans. Getting through the day or the week is often all we can handle. We don't care about the people that don't get it, and we cherish the growing number of people who do get it and don't judge or question us anymore.

Our path has been unusual but we also know that we are not alone. There are many couples and families out there doing their best to cope with their own flavor variety of psychiatric or medical 'abnormalities'. If you are part of this club that no one wants to join, you are not alone either. As much as it feels lonely when no one calls or comes to visit or help, there are many of us suffering silently and doing the best we can, one day at a time.

If you are blessed to NOT to be part of the club, be thankful. Open your hearts and set aside expectations and judgment if you can. Those of us in the club are trying to live in the world of high standards that puts so much pressure on us to be normal – whatever that is. Whew, it's exhausting just to think about how much effort we have to expend, to appear normal and not be judged. It is quite draining. Our society does not have much patience for those with physical or mental limitations. Thanks for listening to me get up on my soapbox.

We have experienced both miracles and hell, everything in between. The most important result of all this, is a deeper level of faith. Our faith would not be this strong and important in our lives if not for the mayhem and sleepless nights, weeks, and years. I would not want to go through it all again, but if it took all that hardship to bring us this close to the Father, the Son and the Holy Spirit, -- well then, I thank God for his persistence in getting our attention.

Life has not become so much easier, but our faith is now the foundation that allows us to look at things with hope and going to the Bible often for answers. Those people who know us would tell you that we are still challenged to not get upset with God at times. Keeping focus on our faith when we're exhausted and can't see straight does not always happen, but we more quickly go back to our foundation than ever before. When we stray off the path, we are guided back on track by a force that we trust. The outside world is too often the last place where compassionate help or understanding can be found when it comes to mental illness.

With that said, we are blessed and thankful to again have each other to lean on. We can figure things out as a team instead of alone. Only the two of us know what we have been through and accept each other's mood swings and imperfections in ways that no one else would. Yes, there is our relationship with Jesus. But face it, sometimes you need an earthly person in the room for validation or to vent to, or just to hug. I am also extremely thankful for the support of my parents who have helped in numerous ways, so many times I can't count. They may not have really understood what was going on at times, but they knew when I would hit my limit of stress and needed a life preserver.

Being the Spouse – Like Working a Second Job

My perspective in the role of spouse and caretaker is a bit overlooked. For a long time I was bitter about being invisible and left alone in the sheer hell of mood swings, hospital visits, too often funeral planning in my head because things were so dire. So many things to manage or understand with little or no guidance. It takes a toll to be in so many roles at one time on top of working full time so that we could financially keep afloat. Everyone asks how John is doing at these times. On rare occasion do people ask how I am doing or offer to help. My mental mantra for many years was "and who takes care of me?" When I started paying attention to the still small voice of God saying "I already am", that made the difference and calmed me. Well, much of the time.

Someone once told me, "no one brings a casserole or baked goods, sends a card, or visits the hospital when someone has a mental illness". Sadly, this is true. Not only that, but people don't want to talk about it if you initiate the topic. People are so uncomfortable, they either begin to avoid you or cut you off and change the topic. There is still too much stigma and fear in our society.

It is my personal opinion that mental illness is much worse than a medical problem. If someone has a medical problem, you can explain their options, have their cooperation in care or decision making. The patient can understand what is happening to them. When mental illness takes hold of one's brain and behavior, there is no cooperation or reasoning, and little correct reporting by the ill person of what's going on within them, or around them.

The amount of guessing that must go on with the professionals that have to struggle to determine how to stabilize or control a very uncontrollable situation is in itself crazy. They are dealing with a person who, at times, truly does not realize they are ill. And, contrary to popular belief, it is not always denial or manipulation on the part of the ill person. There is a word for this, anosognosia, meaning one's lack awareness of their own psychiatric, medical or other condition.

Trying to Ride the Roller Coaster
John's life, for almost ten years, was either a medical or psychiatric crisis, one after another, every 6 to 12 months. It was like riding a roller coaster that may slow down from time to time but revs up and drops over a crest when you least expect it and never really stops to let you off. I have not yet

found a word which describes the hopelessness that can come from not being able to get off that ride once in awhile.

When I married John, I married a man with a sweet and gentle spirit, and a good heart. I had not initially recognized him as a godly man. That was not my thinking process back then. I now know this to be true, and that's part of what I was seeing in him without knowing it. I know that my faith would not be what it is today without John's persistence and gentle way of bringing me to understand and fully accept Christ into my life.

So, in my mid 30's I had stopped looking for a man with great success, material possessions, or a certain look. My experience unfortunately has been that these things can come with too many trappings, expectations or baggage. I felt safe with John. He has ambitions and a high work ethic, but has always been grounded in simple ways of looking at life. What I did not see or know while we dated or agreed to marry was what I was getting into with his bipolar disorder.

It was explained to me by one of his family members casually as "it's like diabetes, he takes his medications, and all is well". That was the extent of the discussion on it prior to our marriage and after. I look at that statement now and I had no idea then that even diabetes requires more management that just taking a pill for most people.

Oh man, the life-long management of a severe mental illness is so damn complicated. Even after being with John for 16 years as I write this, I know full well that we have not figured it all out. We know we must take things as they come, and be extremely hyper-vigilant of any medication change, psychiatric or otherwise. We have to be careful of medical treatments, avoid stress at all costs. Heck, he ended up in a psych hospital with a strangely quick onset mania because of an extreme overdose of vitamin D. It was recommended by a well-meaning MD who was prescribing that to all his patients.

Always on the lookout, always asking questions. We know that even with all that, some strange circumstance or complication can blind-side us when we take a moment to relax. Indeed, it has become our new normal and we have made peace with it, again by leaning on our faith. No person on this earth can really understand and support us in the way we need, and God can.

In most of our strange experiences, I later see God's hand watching over us, either manipulating circumstances or keeping me calm when that is not my nature under duress. In 2008 at what I call the cuckoo's nest hospital, is a great example. I was waiting with John in the emergency intake lobby of a local psych hospital, it was his birthday. We were supposed to be at a Brewer's game and a pool party/barbeque at his parent's house on this warm summer day. We waited in the dark dirty area for over eight hours. The chairs were broken down, the water fountain didn't work, neither did the air conditioning. We were ignored for hours at a time. If not for my walking right up to a staff member, sometimes having to walk behind into areas where I certainly was not supposed to be, maybe we would have been there for days. I just wanted to know what was going on, and all they would say was to be patient and wait. Really, eight hours?

There were only a few people there. The scene was a room with unstable mentally ill folks, some with injuries as well. They were not offered food or water. They sat in a hot room, ignored for hours, not given even a look in their direction as they sat. Some spun more out of control as they waited. I thought I was on some sick version of Candid Camera that was not funny at all. The conditions were ripe for someone to lose it, I thought it might be me. God kept me calm, the time passed. I reached out a few times to John's family who was supposed to be waiting for an update call from us. Many calls, no answers. We were later told that they were having John's birthday party at the pool, grilling and eating without us. We felt so abandoned.

In the evening, after a day of waiting, John was told he would be sent to another nearby psych hospital that was covered by his insurance. John's family refused to bring my car to me from the party as had been previously arranged. I elected to go with John to the other hospital and make sure he was checked in there and then walk home if necessary. It was a few miles from our home. Not desirable as exhausted as I was, but it was doable.

John and I and another patient were loaded like cargo into a vehicle that had the back seat fashioned as a human cage with leather straps instead of metal bars. It was not big enough for one person, and you could not sit upright. It looked like a long low cage for a large dog. Good thing the other patient was a small petite woman as we had to kind of wrap ourselves around each other's upper bodies while folded over at the waist, our heads crushed against the top of the cage. Again God kept all of us calm. It was still over 90 degrees even late at night and we were left to sit in this hot locked vehicle for 15-20 minutes. We sat wrapped like sardines in a can while we had to watch the drivers stand and do their paperwork and on the hood of the vehicle and shoot the bull while we melted. If any one of us would have given in to anxiety, panic or otherwise, well I don't want to think that far.

John's parents did hear the phone messages that I left, and they met us at the other hospital with some of the left over food. They took me back to their place where my car was. It was about 1 am when I got in my car and drove myself home and I collapsed. God protected us from so much that day.

Is it God or Demon?

Was I married to a man possessed of godly spirit or a demonic force? Being in the tornado of someone's psychotic behavior will make you wonder. In the many years before I better had a clue about bipolar, I thought maybe mental illness was the work of the devil. Now that I work in the mental health field and have more education on the matter, I am finding more and more experts making this same connection and using faith to help clients cope.

When I became more involved in learning the Bible, I saw numerous mentions of Satan's actions in the stories and lessons there. Satan struck Job with so much adversity. His property was taken, children killed, and Satan struck his body with boils from head to toe even though Job was a righteous man. Satan was the one who led Adam and Eve astray. My thoughts may not be so far off after all. – Does mental illness have a dark source? I don't think it matters.

The word 'scary' applies more appropriately than 'crazy' for John's appearance when he is psychotically manic. I wish I had a photo of this, even memories of it are creepy. His eyes bug out of his face, so much so that you see too much of the whites of his eyes. You sense something sinister, not John, is inside him. Then you add the erratic fast talking and impulsive behavior on top of minimal bathing and often wearing dirty clothes and bedroom slippers instead of shoes. He looks like something out of a poorly made horror film, or someone who lives on the street.

The first time I witnessed this, I did not sleep for days. I had come home from a seminar out of town. John was not home when I called him to pick me up at the airport, so that was odd. When I was able to get home, he was not there. He showed up a few hours later as I was climbing in bed to watch TV.

He walked in the bedroom with that freak look on his face. He told me that he had filed for divorce and was moving out, then walked out the back door. This was a total surprise, it had not be discussed previously, and not expected. I was not sure if I was more in shock by what he said or by his appearance. He also had not shaved or changed his clothes for days, smelled of alcohol and pot, and was wearing a T-shirt that I later found out he bought from a gas station. On it was the face of a tiger with it's jaws open, and it was so realistic 3-D and took up the entire front of the t-shirt. This just added to the whole freaky visual of the situation, on top of which he had actually lost weight in the week that I was gone and was gaunt in the face. Demonic is the only description I can think of.

By the time I could catch my breath and respond, he was driving away. This was in 2001 and we did not have cell phones yet. There was no way for me to contact him. Nice to meet you mental illness, this was my first dose of mania. I had no idea who to call or what to do. At first I thought it was behavior from the alcohol or pot or some other drug, because I had no frame of reference for mental illness.

It took weeks before I showed up outside his psychiatrist's door demanding help. The psychiatrist said that he could not talk to me because when we got married, John did not sign a release for me to talk with the psychiatrist and be part of John's care. The psychiatrist never suggested that John do this in the first place, we had no idea this was necessary to even initiate it ourselves. Most patients don't know that this is a necessary administrative task to include loved ones in their psychiatric or psychological care.

Lesson – Psychiatrists don't always educate their patients, and often are NOT interested in helping you when you are in a crisis. It's ok to show up for your medication updates and collecting your prescriptions. Beyond that, please do not bother them when the shit really hits the fan and their expertise is really needed. I had no idea where to turn. By this time there were concerns for John's health and safety after weeks of him walking and driving miles to nowhere, after weeks of no sleep and no food.

He had moved out of the house. When John is manic, he has superhuman strength, something else to add to the freak factor. This skinny, weak man with his eyes bugging out of his head lifted furniture items into his van that I thought needed two people. John was very strong in those days but he is tall and very thin, I was sure he would hurt himself. In no time he had moved out and set up an apartment where he used his only remaining income to pay for two months rent.

Thankfully, he rented from a friend of ours who owned apartment buildings, so when it came time to move out, things were worked out easily. Another blessing from God.

What Symptoms Look Like from My Perspective
The low grade mania that I endured for many years was very strange. I can see how some people go undiagnosed or

don't get medications if this is how they live. It will drive everyone around them nuts, but they think things are fine and that anything not right is the other person's problem.

For a long time I thought I was losing my own mind when he would pick fights about little things for no reason. I later learned this is part of the illness. For a long time I thought I was causing it or not doing something right that I just could not figure out. The more I could not figure it out, the angrier I got.

Then there were the years when he was smoking pot and I had no idea. My sense of smell is very keen, never smelled it. I confronted him many times about being high, what kind of denial was I in that I don't know or didn't push the issue. That is not my nature, I chew on things and call them out.

For a long time I thought the lies and manipulative behavior were calculated and intentional to drive me nuts or a sick game that he gained some satisfaction from. Not only learning about bipolar, but most importantly seeing John on the right combination of medications has been eye opening. It has allowed me to see that so much of the strange behavior that got under my skin was not intentional and no longer happens since he's been stabilized on the right medications.

The affairs, the addictive behaviors, impulsive spending. I could write my own book about being on the outside rim of the tornado that is manic behavior.

As a spouse who took the marriage vows very seriously, I wanted to help my spouse, who was mentally or medically struggling. In trying to decide when and how to put up with this, and not put up with that – I am sure I went in and out of being a codependent enabler at times. I learned more about codependency over time. What I learned empowered me to choose my actions, when it would be necessary to be somewhat co-dependent, and when to say no or walk away. Not an exact science, that's for sure.

Business Ventures That Drove Me Nuts

Carpet cleaning – John has opened and closed his carpet cleaning ventures three times, one after theft of the van with everything in it. We could never prove it, but we all knew it was an employee with a criminal record who was involved. John was so good at many aspects of the business. His customers appreciated the perfectionist that he was. He had a high work ethic, but his employees did not. During the years when he ran the company from our basement, I had to deal with the unsavory characters in and out of our house at all hours.

As much as John tried, it was impossible to hire people like himself. They were either late, or under the influence, stole from him or cut corners on the work when he wasn't on a job to supervise. I will never forget the time I drove by an adult video store and the company van was parked there. I knew John was elsewhere for the day, so it was one of the employees. Sure enough, the employee was using the van for personal business and later it was discovered that he used the company credit card for personal purchases.

Whenever John was ill or hospitalized, I would have to help run the business and I hated it. He loved his business but only a few years did it make a profit that allowed him a salary. I often had to give him money to make payroll or pay for an equipment or vehicle repair with money we didn't have.

God made the best of all of it. During all the hospitalizations it helped John know that he could look forward to running the business that he loved after recovery. He would have surely been let go from numerous jobs during those years.

Get Rich Quick Schemes and Network Marketing

I wish I could remember all the network marketing and other get-rich quick type businesses he was involved in. Some were actually good companies with good products. It was a long time before I was educated that getting involved in business schemes is part of bipolar behavior. There were many products including household products, gas pills for better gas mileage, buying and selling retail inventories for a commission, air purifier machines, and the list went on. He purchased an auto-dial phone system that he thought would make cold calls for him to get more new business. That was a $20,000 that was a piece of junk. We had to have an attorney deal with that iron-clad contract when we filed bankruptcy. I grew weary of it all.

Music Ventures

Over the years there have been promotional recordings where John gets musicians together and records music. He uses copies to promote them for future gigs. The recordings have been quite good, one was traditional jazz and the other Christian jazz. The gigs have been few over the years, but well done. A couple of times he has tried to create music events that were attempted during manic episodes. The events did not happen, the musicians were angry.

I Love John, I Hate His Mental Illness

John has been blessed in many ways, one is that he has stayed youthfully handsome in his mid 50's. Unfortunately, there is such a complicated blend of pain, sadness, and peace underneath it all. Some days he looks like death warmed over, some days he looks like the same handsome man I fell in love with in 1996.

On those good days, I suspect that people would not guess the hell he has endured and the daily struggles. At this time, John's daily level of pain is the main challenge. He sleeps a lot, so that when he is awake he can function with minimal pain. His priority in life is taking care of himself, so when he is able to work or volunteer, that he is able to. He has made peace with his limitations in ways that I never suspected he would.

I love John. When I filed for divorce, I wanted to be divorced from his mental illness, not from him. We sat in the waiting area in the divorce court and held hands, and I could not fight back tears when talking to the judge. The mental illness was running our lives, I just could not take it anymore.

When John lost everything during a horrible manic episode in 2010, it seemed like the right thing to do, to have him come back to our house. We had initially applied for low income housing places for him to eventually move out. After about six months, it seemed appropriate and natural for us to stay together. We replaced his wedding ring for Christmas that year and we have worn them ever since. We are getting along much better than when we were married. Only God can do that.

Let us therefore come boldly to the throne of grace,
That we may obtain mercy and find grace
to help in time of need.
Hebrews 4:16

Chapter 13: Godly Relationships --
Earthly People Who Save Your Butt

For where two or three are gathered together in
My name, I am there in the midst of them.
Matthew 18:20

What Are Godly Relationships?
There is one place I can go every day, my Bible. There I can read stories about men and women just like me. I read about how these people find comfort when Jesus shares His knowledge, wisdom, encouragement and healing. He is guiding us into the paths He wants us to take with each other.

I sense that God wants our lives to include three things. He wants us to honor only him, believing in one God. He also wants us to have loving, meaningful relationships, and for us to walk obediently before him and in these relationships. Godly relationships exist when I can talk about my faith with someone, and be understood. Godly relationships exist when someone accepts me as I am and does not judge me or walk away when I am ill. It's not complicated to describe, but can be rare to find.

Doing Business With Godly People
I have two clients, who I now call friends. I have worked with them for many years. They are both godly men, and I could tell from the start. One is a deacon in his church, which I did not know until recently. He teases me, calling me pastor John because of my e-mail ministry and my volunteer chaplain work at the hospital. The other man is a genuine man with the glow of a godly smile that will put your day right every time. These men continue to work with me and accept me as I am when most people have gone running the other direction.

These two special people were clients first and friends later. The spirit-filled foundation of who they are is what has kept them in my life. Both men have seen me through some pretty strange manic behavior, and physical illnesses. I have disappointed them at times during such episodes. Without knowing much about mental illness, both have forgiven me and continued to work with me. These two men deal with large amounts of stress in their very important daily work. One is the manager of a large hotel and conference center, the other handles facilities management for a nearby suburban community.

Most people say in business that you don't just show up at someone's workplace without an appointment. Godly timing was always in play with Daryl and Charles, I rarely had an appointment. My bipolar still makes me impulsive and impatient at times. I would get in the car when the time was right. I would drive to visit Daryl or Charles to schedule work. These extremely busy men would not only be there, but welcomed me with open arms even in the midst of their very hectic day, always time for me. For someone like me who lives with illness, their relationships were not only a source of income, but a source of comfort.

Charles has taught me so much about life in our twelve year relationship. He is a good leader who shares good direction and instruction for me. He also motivates me in almost a fatherly way to lead an obedient Christian life. Ours is a relationship of mutual respect as brothers in Christ.

Daryl is the general manager of a local Hilton Garden Inn Hotel that has been a client of mine for nine years. He has weathered many storms with me as well including business closings and illnesses, yet he continues to support me. I never know when I am going to catch up with him as he rarely answers his cell phone. My habit was to go out to the Hilton, simply on prayer, and he would always appear. He was never in an office, always on the move. No matter where I chose to go: have lunch in the restaurant, walk down a hallway to check the carpeting, or just getting out of my car in the parking lot. I never had to find him, he just appeared every time.

Sometimes I get long winded and I will leave long messages on his cell phone. When I would ask him about it he would always say, "thanks for sharing", instead of berating me for likely filling up his voicemail. Daryl too has gone through suffering which allows him to share compassion and hope. His spirit is filled with his heart. I have been blessed to know Daryl, and I sense the warmth of God's spirit whenever I am in his presence.

I feel such compassion from each of these men. I don't have to feel uncomfortable talking about my faith around them. Rare and wonderful men are Daryl and Charles, with such integrity, and possessing such virtues as detailed in Galatians 5:22-23. I am thankful that these strong Christian forces that have stayed fast in my work life. Truly they are men who display fruits of the spirit.

But the fruit of the Spirit is love, joy, peace, longsuffering, kindness, goodness, faithfulness, gentleness, self-control.
Galatians 5:22-23

I was able to give back in a small way to these men when we gifted them with copies of the small version of the Message Bible that neither had seen before. My wife and I gave away blue copies to men and pink copies to women for a few years as this translation seemed to fit a need for many people we knew.

I have other godly relationships when networking or in work settings. Those connections are special, but they are few. I get different reactions from people. I am never afraid to open my mouth on the subject of my faith. Many people respond and tell me that I make them feel comfortable with it and I am not preachy. I take that as a high compliment. I want to have people be relaxed and open to faith, and not just in church. It is my opinion that God created our businesses, our jobs, our source of income. Why should we not include his presence in this area of our lives by acknowledging it, talking about it, and asking for his help in our work life?

Now prepare yourself like a man;
I will question you, and you shall answer Me.
Job 38: 2-3

There's a Godly Man At The Door
In 2006, Jesus brought a man to our door. He arrived with a gentle smile and a generous spirit. He was also carrying two very special leather-bound Bibles. He came at a time when I was stuck at home in pain, unable to drive. I was spending the summer waiting for my first hernia surgery that was scheduled for September.

This godly man served in a men's ministry with my family church. He supported men in their spiritual needs by visiting them in their homes. My wife and I were unaware of how his visit and my relationship with him would influence my life for years to come.

We had been watching Charles F. Stanley preach every Sunday morning on television since my 2004 pulmonary emboli episode. We have missed few Sunday sermons in the years since. We are touched in immeasurable ways by his sermons, and after all these years we still feel that every sermon is better than the last.

Our visitor came with two leather-bound Charles F. Stanley Life Principles Bibles as gifts. We had seen these and could not afford even one at that time. The gifts brought tears to our eyes, we knew the value of it's contents. These versions include commentary and explanations by Charles Stanley that make it so easy to read and understand the Bible. These Bibles resurrected our lives and our understanding of the Bible. I switched to it and have continued using it in my ministry to this day. For years we purchased the less pricey versions of the Life Principles Bible. We gave dozens away to others who wanted an understandable and simple way to read the Bible.

Our visitor based his life on Jesus with a vast understanding of the scriptures and how to apply them to life. He runs his ministry from Florida, but comes here in the spring and fall to work with the men's ministry. Therefore, my communication over the years with him has been primarily via e-mail. The first couple of years I e-mailed him weekly, asking him questions about the Bible.

My mentor and friend blessed me with a Bible that is on my desk every day, and helped me over the years apply it's principles so that I can even explain things to others. I read that Bible just about every day, sometimes for long periods of time, never getting tired of reading as it is broken up with interesting commentary. His visits, e-mails and encouragement were a part of helping me survive a very difficult period of time. All at once it seemed, my physical health, mental health, the closing of my business, our bankruptcy, and my isolation from the world left me a bit hopeless. He was always there when I needed him. I am blessed and thankful.

But whoever drinks of the water that I shall give him will never thirst. But the water that I shall give him will become in him a fountain of water springing up into everlasting life.
John 4:14

Godly Friendships
I have a special friend who I have known for more than 30 years. He is a very successful attorney, and a very humble and godly man. He helped me out of a business jam back in 1992 and in all of his effort he did not ask to be paid, as he knew I had no money. We have gone to the same church which is where we met. Eric has a great voice and sang in the choir. I liked it when I was playing trombone in the church orchestra and he would have solos where he stood in front of the choir. When he sings, you can feel the presence of God, it's very touching. We attended the same Bible study. I noticed early

on that Eric had a wonderful spirit, sensitive to my bipolar struggles. Back then, I was unstable and unmedicated. This was the worst state in which to build a friendship, but I did the best I could.

I can't remember how many years we have been meeting for lunch almost monthly, but it seems we have done it off and on for many years. I don't get out much, so these lunches are special to me, and lately we have been going to a place located in Miller Park where the Milwaukee Brewers baseball team plays. As we eat our delicious lunch, we overlook the ball field.

Watching the expressions on his face while I tell all my stories is always amusing. I hope he gets as much out of these meetings as I do. I am inspired by the wisdom and wit, and depth of faith in my friend. Eric travels for his job which means he must balance that with his family time with his wife and daughter. He prays and leaves everything on Christ's door step, I am in awe of that.

Eric has a great laugh that I know is sincere, I like to hear it, it makes me feel joy. With Eric, there is a depth of acceptance and no judgment that is part of who he is. But it is something more, he has other people he knows with mental illness, this gives him a unique and generous compassion for me that I am thankful for and appreciate. Focusing on godly friendships like this one enrich my life. He genuinely cares about me and makes me feel like a million bucks. It is my hope that he feels the same way. I love this man for his honesty, he has no airs about him.

In the real world, he is extremely successful and I have almost nothing. In the world of things godly, we are brothers in Christ and on an equal level. That's exactly how he makes me feel. We have equal worth in God's eyes, and I feel that in the way he treats me. God has truly blessed me with this man in my life. He is one of my biggest supporters, which means so much to me when my life is full of people who run far away from me because I am ill. I love you Eric!

Create in me a clean heart, oh God, and renew a steadfast spirit within me. Do not cast me away from Your Presence, and do not take your Holy Spirit from me. Restore to me the joy of Yours salvation.
Psalm 51:10-11

I have a close friend who knows the Lord as I do. We meet every other week or so, and we spend hours talking about God and our lives. I have known him for almost 20 years. We played cards together for many years and met while working for the same company. In recent years we started to meet, just the two of us, to talk. Talking about God is exciting, we challenge each other and our views on life. We encourage each other.

We open the Bible on occasion and one of us will open to the page that is exactly what we needed to hear. What we read matches what we were discussing, as if God is part of the discussion. The conversation between us is never boring. We have had our days in the past when we did not get along, and I wondered if the relationship could be healed. It seems the more we talk about our faith, the deeper and more healed our relationship is. He is a great sounding board I love him very much as a brother. When God is involved, relationships are healed. Godly friendships do not have to start in church, they can start anywhere.

Then there's Kathy, a special woman of faith who I met through my parents. She did some initial editing of this book as her gift to support the project. We communicate mostly through e-mails, she will reply to my e-mail ministry verses and messages. She is always very supportive and when a few months pass she sends an e-mail and wants to know what is going on. She is sensitive to mental illness struggles as she has had experience in the past with depression, and knows others with bipolar disorder too.

She has a master's degree in pastoral care and is an extremely kind and gentle person, the kind of person you want to know. Even with my mental illness, she treats me with respect, not as something less. Thank you Kathy for living by example how to respect others in a godly way.

My Dad

I always stayed in the shadow of my father. Living his life, enjoying his blessings was how I felt. I was the architect's son, I felt proud and in his shadow is where I felt comfortable. I felt close to my father when I was growing up on the farm. It was fun riding the horses and balling the hay. One day dad and I were riding down a field, I was about nine years old. It was slippery conditions and down I went. He was right there to help me back up. Dad was tough, crying was no good. I had to just get back up on the horse. Dad could be tough but I learned from him to suck it up and deal with things. I still have days when crying seems like a better idea.

Dad would never let anything intimidate him, he went gung-ho full on into things and didn't look back. Dad was an architect for 56 years. Before his business closed, Wenzler Architects was awarded in 2008 the first ever Lifetime Service Award from the Governor for service and excellence in design for the State of Wisconsin for 40 years. There is also a scholarship in their name at the UW Milwaukee School of Architecture and Urban Planning, the William P. and Edward W. Wenzler Honorary Scholarship.

Dad has a deep faith he has tried to pass on to me. He would always be reaching out to the poor. I remember he would bring his Sunday school class out to the farm. The church members came from the central city where our church was. He was always trying to save people. Watching him for years has given me a confidence to talk about faith to just about anyone.

I remember how much fun it was to fly with him as the pilot, in the small airplanes that he flew out of state for work. He would let me fly for a little while sometimes. I was actually lucky to be in his shadow, because I could experience things through him that I could never learn or achieve on my own.

When I was only about three years old, dad received a fellowship from the University of Illinois to travel by boat with our family to Europe and study architecture. All we could afford at that time was to live in a tent. Yes, we lived in a tent in Europe with three kids, me still in diapers. My parents had a lot of courage, caring for three children while dad studied for six months. What an opportunity to grow in architecture and design, I admire him for not passing on the opportunity. He and mom found a way to make it work. That's another godly lesson I learned from dad: never give up, find a way.

When my twenties came, things shifted with me and dad as my bipolar swings began. For the first seven years I was unstable, no medications prescribed for me and dad had to pick up the pieces so many times. He would either rescue me from a situation or bail me out financially.

On one occasion, he, my brother, and our pastor picked me up in Rockford, Illinois from jail. Another time it was co-signing a note to pay off all the musicians for a concert, it was always something. Uncontrolled mania was destroying my life, dad must have grown weary picking up the broken pieces of my life. I was a mess and didn't know what to do. Dad and mom changed my psychiatrist after fifteen years of unstable due to little medication being recommended.

Dad always liked boats, he has talked about the canoe he bought when he was 16 years old. Later in my life he bought a 28-ft. sailboat. What a wonderful adventure between us. As adults we found something to share, we really enjoyed ourselves. My mental illness for some reason did not stand in the way of my skill with the sailboat. Dad trusted me to take friends out on the sailboat. He did not trust me with much as an adult because, for the most part I was unstable.

In recent years, with all my physical surgeries, dad and I became friends again. He reads the Bible for a long time each morning and during some of my surgeries he would stay overnight or come in the morning and read it to me. Since mom's death, we have spent so much time together. We talk more often, we meet for lunch every other week. We talk about

God and our faith, I learn from him. We have become much closer, we tell stories and I am learning things about him that I never knew. I am sad that mom is gone, but if it allowed me to have this special relationship with dad, I am thankful. I love you dad!

Honor your father and mother,
which is the first commandment with promise:
that it may be well with you
and you may live long on the earth.
Ephesians 6:2-3

Why Godly Relationships Are Important

The reason I wrote this chapter is because of the importance of godly relationships to my life, my coping with all of my illnesses and limitations. Having so much rejection from people due to my mental illness is frustrating. In focusing on faith-filled relationships, I no longer look to be great friends with everyone. Fewer high quality relationships are so enriching, and I have stopped beating myself up when a relationship does not work. There is no need to have every relationship work out.

Jesus provides opportunity for many godly relationships so I am getting better and leaving the rest behind and not trying so hard to convince people who don't understand or who judge me. It doesn't matter where we came from or what has happened in the past. What is important is where we are at and who thrives in our heart and in our life. Someone asked me once if all my friends are Christians. No not all, but most. When someone says to me that they know Jesus, I know that I am going to truly appreciate our conversation.

Sometimes mentioning the name of Jesus upsets others. People who believe they know Jesus Christ, and have accepted Him in their lives usually have a different air about them that I can pick up on. I like to have a conversation about Jesus, that is what really matters to me. But I have some distant friends who say Jesus is left for church on Sundays. I have been told that God is not in the work place, which I disagree with. We all began somewhere with our faith, and what I like to talk about is the importance of a daily relationship with Jesus. I like to talk with believers or non believers about the Father, Son and Holy Spirit that lives in us. I did not know the riches that God was going to bless me with after my last two month manic episode. Jesus is a very close friend of mine and I want others to know him like I do. He is not lacking for me to want to get to know Him better. It seems I am just learning about His blessings, and when I learn something I like to share it with others.

I try to remember where I was when I talk to others. For example, if I find out that someone would rather lie than tell the truth or be buried in porn or sexual immorality, I remember that I was like that. I try to explain the need to repent and move ahead, and how I suffered too. Not every one is interested, but I plant seeds in people's minds, I try.

My biggest blessing has been reuniting with my ex-wife in 2010, such a godly relationship that we now have, I could not have imagined. We did not have a Godly existence when we were married, we do now and it is heavenly. It is God's handy work that we are together and we never forget how special our existence is because of Him.

If anyone serves Me, let him follow Me;
and where I am, there my servant will be also.
If anyone serves Me, him My Father will honor.
John 12:26

*Beloved, I pray that you may prosper
in all things
and be in health,
just as your soul prospers.*

3 John 2

ABOUT THE AUTHORS

John W. Wenzler

John lives in Milwaukee, Wisconsin where he was raised. Mental illness complicated his life, starting in his teen years. The following years without medications caused extreme mental suffering. Bipolar swings for fifteen years made it impossible for him to keep a steady job. So, he opened his own business which he ran for many years on and off through the ups and downs of his illnesses. Once on a therapeutic level of lithium, John was able to work at the same job for six years as a driver and enjoy a period of normalcy.

In the past decade or so, due to medical conditions, mania was often the result of the stress or medications related to those illnesses. Through it all, John's faith has been tested but remained a foundation of his coping.

John always had faith in God even when his illness was not stable. Now on a new medication and very stable, there is consistency in his faith as he deals with chronic pain daily.

Karrie Wenzler

Karrie was born in Milwaukee, Wisconsin where she now lives with John. She has also lived in Minneapolis, and the San Francisco bay area. She came to Milwaukee for a summer to visit family, met John, and never went back to California.

She recently graduated in 2010 with her master's degree in counseling. She currently works as a mental health social worker and looks forward to being a licensed professional counselor soon. Her experience with John's mental illness led her into the mental health field.

Her passion to help John get his message out to others along with her past knowledge of self-publishing has made this project a team effort and labor of love.

TO ORDER COPIES OF THIS BOOK

*Share the message
with colleagues, friends, family*

To order one or more copies of this book,
go to www.godsgracepublishing.com
for ordering the paperback
or downloadable version

For volume discounts,
contact us by e-mailing:
godsgracepublishing@gmail.com